MANAGING
YOUR
Emotions

MANAGING
YOUR
Emotions

Daily Wisdom for Remaining
Stable in an *Unstable World*

A 90 Day Devotional

JOYCE MEYER

New York • Nashville

FaithWords
Hachette Book Group
1290 Avenue of the Americas, New York, NY 10104
faithwords.com
twitter.com/faithwords

First Edition: October 2023

FaithWords is a division of Hachette Book Group, Inc. The FaithWords name and logo are trademarks of Hachette Book Group, Inc.

The publisher is not responsible for websites (or their content) that are not owned by the publisher.

The Hachette Speakers Bureau provides a wide range of authors for speaking events. To find out more, go to hachettespeakersbureau.com or email HachetteSpeakers@hbgusa.com.

FaithWords books may be purchased in bulk for business, educational, or promotional use. For information, please contact your local bookseller or the Hachette Book Group Special Markets Department at special.markets@hbgusa.com.

Print book interior design by Bart Dawson.

ISBNs: 978-1-5460-2924-3 (paper over board), 978-1-5460-2923-6 (ebook)

Printed in the United States of America

LSC-C

Printing 3, 2024

CONTENTS

INTRODUCTION

If someone were to ask me to share the most important lessons I have learned as a Christian, I would certainly include the way God has taught me that I do not have to let my feelings and emotions control my behavior. I have learned that I can have emotions without letting them have me; in other words, I can live beyond my feelings. Of course, I have also learned many other valuable lessons in my walk with God, but learning to deal with emotions in healthy, godly ways is one that has truly changed me and enabled me to consistently enjoy my life each day and stay stable in an unstable world. I pray that as you spend the next ninety days in this book, thinking and praying about how you deal with your emotions, you will also find yourself enjoying your life in new and wonderful ways as you experience a greater level of emotional stability.

When you wake up each morning, do you wait to see how you feel before you decide what you will do? If so, you won't end up doing much of what you should do. Do you wait to see what you think, and then decide how to spend your day? Or do you use your free will to decide to do what you know you should do? Do you think of something sad that happened the night before and allow your sad feelings to set the tone of the day? Do you allow worry or anxiety to cause you to dread going to work? Do you immediately remember the stress of something that happened earlier in the week? Do you think of a certain person and feel anger, jealousy, or resentment? Perhaps you do at times, but you don't have to let these emotions set the tone for your day. You can change how you feel by changing what you think.

Emotions are part of being human. People express their emotions differently, but we all have them. However, we don't have to let our feelings lead us into unhealthy and unwise decisions. We can choose how to deal with them. Feelings are fickle, and they cannot be trusted. You and I can feel one way when we go to bed and wake up feeling an entirely different way. For example, this morning I went to my gym to exercise and decided I would take a walk when I came back, but after working out, I felt like sitting in a chair for a while.

God's Word encourages us to make good choices in Deuteronomy 30:19: "This day I call the heavens and the earth as witnesses against you that I have set before you life and death, blessings and curses. Now choose life, so that you and your children may live." God gives us two choices: life or death, blessing or curse. He even tells us which one to choose. He says to "choose life," meaning to make decisions that lead to a life filled with His blessings.

We make a life-changing choice to be blessed when we decide to receive Jesus as Savior and Lord. Because God gives us free will (the ability to do what we want to do), we have opportunities to choose to be blessed each day as we make decisions consistent with His Word. On some days, our emotions help us make godly decisions. But on other days they betray us and try to prevent us from making good decisions.

Each day you live can be a good one. This, of course, doesn't mean you will not face situations that affect your emotions. You may find yourself in a circumstance that makes you extremely happy and fills your heart with joy. Or something may happen to anger you, frighten you, or sadden you. You have no control over many things you deal with each day, but you do get to determine how you respond to them. You can't choose what happens to you, but you have complete control over how you decide to deal with it. You do not have to feel like doing the right thing in order to choose to do it. You can live beyond your emotions.

I pray this devotional will encourage and empower you to enjoy every day of your life as you choose to manage your emotions regarding people and situations instead of letting your emotions manage you.

MANAGING
YOUR
Emotions

It's Your Choice

---

*This day I call the heavens and the earth as witnesses
against you that I have set before you life
and death, blessings and curses. Now choose life,
so that you and your children may live.*

Deuteronomy 30:19

As you begin this ninety-day journey of learning to manage your emotions more effectively so you can be stable in an unstable world, it's important to realize that no one is born knowing how to manage their emotions, but we can learn to do it. Making healthy, godly decisions when we feel like doing something else is vital to enjoying a victorious life. For years, I simply did what I felt like doing, and it got me into a lot of trouble. But God has taught me how to follow His Word instead of following my emotions. I don't always succeed, but I have learned a lot about this and will continue learning all of my life.

People respond to emotions in various ways.

Some ignore, deny, or suppress their feelings. Others respond physically—by overeating, drinking, exercising excessively, or substance abuse (whether that's sugar, caffeine, prescription medications, or mood-altering drugs). Still others withdraw when emotions are intense, while others run to their friends or to social media to process how they feel. And there are some who go on cleaning sprees, and others take shopping trips. The list goes on. Perhaps you've experienced one or more of these unhealthy responses. If so, today is the day you can begin to handle your emotions in positive ways instead of negative ones.

In today's scripture, God tells His people to "choose life." This means to make decisions that lead to peace, joy, and stability. We learn how to make these decisions as we study His Word, and we find peace, joy, and stability as we obey it.

———————

Prayer: *Thank You, God, for Your Word and for the ways it teaches me to choose life. Help me to obey it in every area of my life for as long as I live.*

Decide to Enjoy Your Day

---

*This is the day the Lord has made;
we will rejoice and be glad in it.*
Psalm 118:24 NKJV

As I mentioned in the introduction, learning to manage my emotions has been one of the most important lessons I have learned in my journey with God, because it has allowed me to consistently enjoy my life. When we wait to see how we feel before we know if we can enjoy each day, we give emotions control over our lives. But thankfully, we can make decisions that are not based on feelings. If we are willing to make good choices regardless of how we feel, God will be faithful to help us do so.

Living the good life that God offers us requires us to be obedient to His way of being and doing. He gives us the strength to follow His teachings, but we must choose to do it. God won't choose for us. He helps us, but we must participate by choosing to obey His Word instead of simply doing whatever we feel like doing. We can't consistently enjoy life until we are willing to do this. For example, I may feel like avoiding someone because they have hurt my feelings or treated me unfairly, but I can choose to pray for them and treat them as Jesus would while I wait for Him to do something in that situation. If I act according to my feelings, I will forfeit peace and joy. But if I choose to do what God has instructed me to do in His Word, I will have His reward and blessing in my life.

———————

Prayer: *Help me, God, to make good choices regarding my emotions and not to allow them to control my life. I want to obey Your Word and experience Your blessings in my life.*

DAY 3

You Are Loved and Accepted

---

*God made him who had no sin to be sin
for us, so that in him we might
become the righteousness of God.*

2 Corinthians 5:21

God wants us to feel loved and accepted. This is why His Word includes so many scriptures that remind us of His unconditional love for us (John 3:16, 15:13; Romans 8:35–39). According to Romans 5:8, while we were still sinners and before we cared anything about God, He sent His Son to die for us, to pay the price for our sins, and to make a way for us to live in close fellowship with Him.

When we receive Jesus as our Savior, He takes our sin and gives us His righteousness, as today's scripture teaches us. We may not understand the full impact of this. How can we fathom what it really means to be made right with God at no cost to ourselves? This is a glorious truth, one that will change the way we see ourselves as it sinks into our hearts.

I challenge you today to believe that God loves and accepts you completely, that He thinks highly of you, and that you are rightly related to Him through Christ. Think a positive thought about yourself or speak a positive word about yourself based on how God feels about you. I'm not talking about being in pride, but I am encouraging you to be bold enough to believe you really are who God says you are.

David says to God in Psalm 139:14, "I praise you because I am fearfully and wonderfully made; your works are wonderful, I know that full well." Many people struggle to believe such positive words about themselves, but I hope and pray today that you will believe them for yourself, because they are true.

Prayer: *Thank You, Lord, for loving and accepting me completely and for making me righteous through Christ. Help me to feel about myself the way You feel about me.*

How to Talk about How You Feel

When there are many words, transgression and offense are unavoidable, but he who controls his lips and keeps thoughtful silence is wise.

Proverbs 10:19 AMP

People tend to talk a lot about how they feel. Some talk about their feelings more than almost anything else. They feel good or bad, happy or sad, excited or discouraged, fearful or bold, stressed or at ease, loved or unloved, angry or peaceful, jealous or happy when others succeed or are blessed. The list of adjectives that describe emotions is almost endless.

Feelings are ever changing, usually without notice, doing as they please for no specific reason. We have all experienced going to bed feeling fine physically and emotionally only to wake up the next morning feeling tired and irritable. We often tell anyone who will listen how we feel and say much more about our negative feelings than we do our positive ones. If I wake up feeling energetic and excited about the day, I rarely announce it. But if I feel tired and discouraged, I want to tell everyone. It has taken me years to learn that talking about how I feel increases the intensity of those feelings, so it seems to me that we should talk about our positive ones and keep quiet about the negative feelings.

We can always tell God how we feel and ask for His help and strength, but talking about negative feelings just to be talking does no good. If negative feelings persist, asking for prayer or seeking advice can be helpful, but again I want to stress that talking just to be talking is useless. Even if you say, "I feel tired," you can follow it with "but I believe God will energize me." When you talk about how you feel, speak positively.

———————

Prayer: *Lord, today I want to use wisdom as I speak about my emotions. Help me to talk about my positive feelings so they will grow and to keep quiet about my negative feelings, as I trust You to help me with them.*

DAY 5

Choose Faith

Be on your guard; stand firm in the faith;
be courageous; be strong.
1 Corinthians 16:13

We can conquer fear with faith. When our thoughts tell us "You can't," we should remember that God says "You can" and echo Paul's declaration in Philippians 4:13: "I can do all things through Christ who strengthens me" (NKJV). Even when we feel fear, we can move forward in faith, knowing that Christ is in us and we are in Him.

When Peter saw Jesus walking on water and wanted to do the same, he climbed out of the boat and began taking steps. As long as he kept his eyes on Jesus, he did indeed walk on water. But when he focused on the waves around him, he grew frightened and started to sink. Jesus reached out and saved him, but He also lovingly rebuked him for his great fear and his little faith (Matthew 14:25–31). Peter could have chosen faith and continued walking on water, but he chose fear instead, and Jesus had to rescue him. The feeling of fear will never completely disappear from our lives, but whatever we need to do, we can "do it afraid" and be courageous as we keep our eyes on Jesus. Courage is not the absence of fear; it is confronting and mastering fear.

Sometimes we don't see how we could possibly have faith, but these are the times we must refuse to follow fear, with God's help.

God never stops loving us and doesn't become angry with us because we choose fear, but it does make Him sad, because He wants us to live the best life we can live. Throughout His Word, He instructs us not to fear, and He will give us the grace and strength to do it.

Prayer: *Thank You, God, for the gift of faith. When I am tempted to be afraid, help me choose faith instead.*

DAY 6

You Have Authority over Your Emotions

---

*Like a city whose walls are broken through
is a person who lacks self-control.*

Proverbs 25:28

Feelings in and of themselves are neither good nor evil. They are, however, unstable and unpredictable at times, so they need to be managed. They can be enjoyable and wonderful, but they can also make us miserable and drive us to make choices we eventually regret. Unbridled emotions can be compared to young children who want to have and do everything but don't understand that some things can be dangerous. Parents must control their children, or they will surely hurt themselves or others. Similarly, we can learn to "parent" our emotions. We need to train them to avoid dangerous and unhealthy situations and to live the life and blessings God has for us.

Understanding our feelings is important, but not nearly as important as controlling them and not allowing them to run wild. Just as parents have authority over their children, you have authority over your emotions. You can decide that you will no longer let them control you.

The way you manage your emotions will determine how you live your life—whether you are a victim or a victor, whether you go forward in confidence or shrink back in fear when great opportunities present themselves, and whether you become known as a peacemaker or as a person who stirs up strife.

Feelings can be strong and demand their own way, but you don't have to let them have it. Choosing to handle them well can position you to receive and enjoy the best God has for you each day, in every situation you face.

———————

Prayer: *Help me, God, to manage my emotions in ways that position me to receive the best You have for me today.*

A Key to Emotional Health

*Bear with each other and forgive one another
if any of you has a grievance against someone.
Forgive as the Lord forgave you.*

Colossians 3:13

I believe one reason many people live in emotional turmoil is that they refuse to forgive people who have hurt or wronged them. Whether we realize it or not, unforgiveness is often the root of negative feelings. Many people feel justified and think they have a right to refuse to forgive. They think they should hurt the people who hurt them. But this isn't emotionally healthy or wise.

Very painful things can happen to us in life. Many times, the key to getting through them and being able to enjoy our lives in the future is learning to forgive what has happened in the past. I'm convinced that, as believers and followers of Christ, we will never experience joy-filled, victorious lives unless we forgive people.

Forgiveness is not a feeling; it's a choice. We can choose to forgive someone whether we feel like it or not. We can even choose to forgive while we feel angry or hurt. Once we make the decision to forgive, our emotions eventually calm down. As we continue to walk in forgiveness, hurt and anger subside. We may not choose to restore our relationship with the person who hurt us, but forgiveness sets us free from negative feelings toward them and may eventually lead us to feel compassion for them. When we forgive people, we can bless them and pray for them, as Jesus teaches. As a result, we will be blessed too. We don't know all the blessings that will come from forgiveness, but we do know it will lead to peace in our hearts and that it's a key to emotional health.

Prayer: *God, help me choose to forgive everyone who has hurt or wronged me, even when I don't feel like forgiving them.*

Fight in God's Strength

---

*He said: "Listen, King Jehoshaphat and all who live in
Judah and Jerusalem! This is what the Lord says to you:
'Do not be afraid or discouraged because of this vast
army. For the battle is not yours, but God's.'"*
2 Chronicles 20:15

Are you asking God for something or believing that
He will fulfill a promise He has made? During
times like this, we can be tempted to believe that once
God does what we are believing Him to do, everything will be wonderful and we will have no more
problems. But trusting God often means facing obsta-
cles to our breakthrough and taking steps of faith.

We would be wise to remember how God led the
Israelites into the Promised Land. After they crossed
the Jordan River, their journey was not easy. They had
to fight one enemy after another. As they learned to
lean on God and His strength, not relying on their
human abilities, they were victorious.

When you're filled with hope and faith that God's going to do something wonderful in your life, it's natural to feel happy and excited. But if you face an unexpected obstacle, you may be discouraged. If the obstacle is big, you may even want to give up at times.

When things get difficult as you move toward God's promises, remember the Israelites, and don't let the battles intimidate you. If something becomes difficult or frustrating, it doesn't mean God isn't leading you. He may take you through a test or trial so you can grow stronger or demonstrate your faith. He may be maturing you spiritually so you will be able to handle the blessings He wants to bring into your life.

Anytime you face a battle, remember that the battle belongs to the Lord. God will not only strengthen you in the midst of difficulty, but He will also fight for you.

Prayer: *Lord, when I face various battles, help me not to rely on my own strength but to lean on You and Your strength, remembering that You fight for me.*

The Truth Will Set You Free

---

*You will know the truth, and the truth
will set you free.*

John 8:32

The words of today's scripture are so important because of the way they apply to emotional health and stability. A person with a history of out-of-balance emotional behavior may act the way they do because they've not faced the truth about certain issues in their lives, perhaps even long-standing problems rooted in their childhood. They're not free but are still captive to the negative things that happened to them. Until they confront the painful issues from their past, they won't begin to heal and move into emotional wholeness and freedom. Confrontation isn't easy, but it's easier than remaining in bondage all your life.

My father sexually abused me. I thought moving away from him would solve the problem. But several years passed before I realized that the abuse was still affecting my personality and the ways I dealt with everyone and everything in my life. I carried heavy burdens of fear, shame, and anxiety. My journey of healing began when I was willing to confront the pain inside me and to deal with the problems it was causing in my life.

I eventually learned that hurting people hurt people, and I was able to forgive my father. I realized that what happened to me didn't have to define who I was. My past could not control my future unless I allowed it to. I needed a great work of healing in my soul, and as I faced the truth about what had happened to me, God brought healing, wholeness, and freedom to my life. He will do the same for you.

Prayer: *Lord, show me the truth about the situations that cause me pain and problems. Help me face it, so I can be set free.*

You Don't Have to Feel Overwhelmed

Moses' father-in-law replied, "What you are doing is not good. You and these people who come to you will only wear yourselves out. The work is too heavy for you; you cannot handle it alone."

Exodus 18:17–18

M oses was a very busy man, to the point of being overwhelmed and stressed. As the leader of the children of Israel, he had many responsibilities and a lot to think about. The people looked to him to settle their disputes, solve their problems, give them advice, and provide help in many other ways. Finally, his father-in-law, Jethro, told him the work was too much for him to handle alone and helped him learn to delegate some of his responsibilities.

As you read about Moses and his father-in-law, maybe you're thinking, *I can relate!* Maybe you, too, feel overwhelmed. Perhaps the responsibilities you carry have become too heavy and you don't feel you can continue to handle them by yourself.

Being too stressed and overwhelmed is something we all face and need to manage at times. We can approach this several different ways. We can take care of ourselves physically, making sure to eat right, exercise, and sleep enough. We can seek support from the people around us. We can learn to set healthy boundaries and say no to certain things. And best of all, we can ask God to help us.

He may lead us to delegate certain tasks, give us insight into ways we can be more efficient, or give us creative ways to manage our stress. According to John 14:26, the Holy Spirit is our Helper, and we can call on Him at any time in any situation. We can be sure that when we ask, He will help us.

Prayer: *Lord, help me know what to do when I feel overwhelmed, and send me the help I need.*

A Peaceful Home Base

When you enter a house, first say, "Peace to this house."
If someone who promotes peace is there, your peace
will rest on them; if not, it will return to you.
Stay there, eating and drinking whatever they
give you, for the worker deserves his wages.
Do not move around from house to house.

Luke 10:5-7

During Jesus' earthly ministry, He sent some of His followers out two by two to do His kingdom work. He said to them, basically, "Go and find a house and say, 'Peace be unto you.' And if your peace settles on that house, then you can stay there. If it doesn't, shake the dust off your feet and go on" (Matthew 10:12–14; Luke 10:5–11).

At one time in my life, I felt repeatedly drawn to these scriptures, and I didn't know why. I finally realized that God was trying to help me understand what Jesus was saying to His disciples in today's scripture. I needed to learn that in order to minister with His anointing (the grace and power of the Holy Spirit in me), I needed to live in peace.

As I continued to study and meditate on these verses, I realized that in order to serve Him most effectively, all of us need a peaceful base of operations, a place from which we can go out and to which we can go back. For most of us, this place is our home. If our homes aren't peaceful, we need to do whatever we can to gain and maintain a calm, peaceful atmosphere, because strife and confusion adversely affect the anointing of God that rests on our lives. Even if you can't have peace in your home because the other people refuse to be peaceful, you can remain peaceful in your heart.

Let me encourage you to do all you can do to ensure peace in your "home base." That way, everyone who lives and works from that place will do so with God's grace and peace—and they will have success.

———————

Prayer: *Lord, show me anything I need to do to establish and maintain peace in my home, and help me create a peaceful atmosphere for all who live there, including myself.*

God Restores the Soul

The Lord is my shepherd; I shall not want.
He makes me to lie down in green pastures;
He leads me beside the still waters.
He restores my soul; He leads me in the paths
of righteousness for His name's sake.

Psalm 23:1–3 NKJV

Today's scripture reminds us that the Lord is our shepherd. This means He watches over us and leads us to where we should go. Because He cares for us as a shepherd cares for his sheep, He provides everything we need. This doesn't mean we get to have every single thing we want or that we don't lack anything we desire. It means that all our needs are met. We lack nothing we truly need.

The Lord, as our shepherd, makes us "lie down in green pastures" and leads us "beside the still waters." This is the place where we can finally stop running from the pain of the past and decide to face it—to receive the emotional healing and spiritual and emotional rest God offers us.

God is not only a shepherd and a healer; He's also a restorer. He promises to restore our souls. The soul is comprised of the mind, the will, and the emotions. He will heal and restore all that is wounded, sick, or broken in our souls if we ask for His help and cooperate with His healing process in our lives. When we spend time with God in His Word and in His presence, we learn that He offers us a new life, one filled with wholeness. When the soul is healthy and restored, we experience joy and peace, and everything in life goes better for us. Please be encouraged that you will be restored if you invite God into the wounded places in your soul.

Prayer: *Thank You, God, for being my shepherd, my healer, and my restorer. In You, I have everything I need. Restore my soul today, I pray.*

Take Care of Yourself

---

*Dear friend, I pray that you may enjoy
good health and that all may go well with you,
even as your soul is getting along well.*

3 John 2

Sometimes we experience hardships, such as the loss of a loved one or betrayal of a close friend, that impact our life in devastating ways. I've discovered from my own experiences that when you are going through a prolonged season of deep painful emotions, especially grief, it is important to realize that you may need to do some things differently to manage the stress and intensity of your feelings. Taking care of yourself and your own needs will help you get through the situation in a healthy way.

Taking care of yourself means different things to different people. For some it may mean taking a few days of paid time off to take a break from a toxic work environment or scheduling a massage or manicure on a regular basis for a while. For others it may mean preparing healthy meals, exercising frequently, and getting enough sleep at night. Introverts may want to spend time reading a book, while extroverts may want to eat lunch with friends or go to a social event. It doesn't matter what the people around you do to take care of themselves. You do what *you* need to do to take care of *yourself*.

Sometimes people feel guilty about taking care of themselves and making sure their needs are met. There is no reason to feel this way. Think of it as doing yourself a favor. Taking care of yourself will not only bless and help you; it will be a blessing to the people who care about you. Because if you don't take care of yourself, you won't be able to take care of anyone else. Always remember during difficult times that good times are on their way.

———————

Prayer: *Lord, help me remember and find creative ways to take care of myself during times of stress and intense emotion.*

DAY 14

Everything You Need

One thing I ask from the Lord, this only do I seek:
that I may dwell in the house of the Lord
all the days of my life, to gaze on the beauty
of the Lord and to seek him in his temple.

Psalm 27:4

Often, our emotions are upset because we want something and do not have it. When we can't seem to get what we want, we can become frustrated, angry, sad, confused, fearful, and envious of those who do have it.

Let me ask you today, if you could ask for only one thing, what would it be? In today's scripture, David's "one thing" is God's presence. More than anything else, David wanted to know God as He really is and to be with Him. When we sense His presence, all other desires fall into their proper place. In His presence we find perfect peace and "fullness of joy" (Psalm 16:11 AMP). Our emotions are stable, happy, and at rest when we are in God's presence.

Unfortunately, we can get so distracted with the rush and pressure of the details of our lives that we neglect the most important thing—spending time in God's presence—and instead chase things that are ultimately not important. How foolish we are to spend our lives seeking things that can't satisfy while we ignore God, the "One Thing" who can give us great joy, peace, satisfaction, and contentment. We never know the joy of seeking the One we really need. An old saying attributed to Blaise Pascal basically says that in every person's heart is a God-shaped vacuum or hole that God alone can fill. No matter what else we try to fill it with, we will remain empty and frustrated.

If you find your emotions on edge today because you want something you don't have, take time to be in God's presence. When you do, you'll find everything you truly need.

———————————

Prayer: *Lord, I repent for seeking things that don't really matter. Help me to find everything I need as I spend time in Your presence.*

Tell Your Emotions to Be Patient

He took him outside and said, "Look up at the sky and count the stars—if indeed you can count them." Then he said to him, "So shall your offspring be."

Genesis 15:5

God promised Abram (later Abraham) a son. Not only that, but He promised him descendants so numerous that they would be like the stars in the sky. The problem was that Abram and his wife, Sarai (later Sarah), were way too old to have natural children. As advanced in years as they were, we might think God's promise needed to come to pass quickly. But it didn't. Abram and Sarai had to wait twenty-five years for His promise to manifest in their lives.

We often have to wait for certain things God has promised to come to pass, just as Abram and Sarai did. Sometimes He may need to teach us or prepare us for the blessings He wants to release in our lives. Or it could be that we need additional spiritual growth, greater emotional stability, or a new mindset before we can handle them properly. While we wait, we may be tempted to feel impatient. We may doubt or feel frustrated because nothing seems to be happening.

During these seasons of waiting for God's promises to be fulfilled, we need to tell our emotions to calm down and wait patiently for Him to act on our behalf. Our emotions can help us wait peacefully, with joy and expectation, or they can keep us anxious and impatient.

God is always working for our good, even when we don't see it. We need to trust His timing and wisdom, knowing He will fulfill His promises at the time that is best for us.

———————

Prayer: *Thank You, God, for the promises You've made to me. I trust You to fulfill them when the time is right. Help me to wait patiently and not let my emotions lead me into frustration.*

Control What's under Your Control

Love bears all things [regardless of what comes],
believes all things [looking for the best in each one],
hopes all things [remaining steadfast during difficult
times], endures all things [without weakening].

1 Corinthians 13:7 AMP

When I think about what stirs up our emotions, the hurtful things people do to us is at the top of the list, perhaps more frequently than anything else. Since we cannot control what others do, we need to look for ways to quiet our emotions when people upset us. The amplification of today's scripture teaches us to look for the best in things, and I believe this applies to people as well as situations.

Our natural thoughts and emotions, without the influence of the Holy Spirit, can be negative. Romans 8:5 teaches us that we can either set our minds on what the flesh (human nature without God) desires or on what the Holy Spirit desires. If we set our minds on the flesh, we will be filled with negative feelings and attitudes. But if we set our minds on the Spirit, we will be filled with life and peace in our souls, which includes calm emotions. I encourage you to choose what creates peace, because a life of emotional turmoil makes us miserable.

I realized years ago that most of my emotional turmoil came from people problems. I knew from experience that I could not control people and what they decided to do, so I began to pray about what I could do to keep their words and actions from upsetting me. In answer to my prayers, and through studying God's Word, I started obeying 1 Corinthians 13:7 by choosing to believe the best of everything and everyone.

Prayer: *Help me, Lord, to control what I can control—my thoughts and emotions—while trusting You to handle what I can't control.*

Don't Let Fear Push You Around

---

*For I am the Lord your God who takes
hold of your right hand and says to you,
Do not fear; I will help you.*

Isaiah 41:13

Fear is everywhere, and everyone has to face it at some point. It's afflicted humanity since the beginning of time, and it will be an emotion people deal with for as long as they live. Although fear will never totally disappear from our lives, we can manage it as we choose to face it and resist it with God's help.

We would be surprised if we realized how often our reactions to people and situations are based on fear. We respond out of fear much more than we think. In fact, some people spend their entire lives allowing fear to dictate their decisions and reactions to circumstances. This keeps them from being who they truly want to be and causes them to feel dissatisfied and unfulfilled.

If you are one of these people, let me encourage you to acknowledge your fear, because it is a real emotion, but also to move forward in spite of it. Courageous people do what they believe in their hearts they should do, no matter how they feel or what kinds of doubts and fearful thoughts fill their minds.

Fear will try to stop you from doing what God has called you to do and what you'd like to do. Don't allow fear to prevent you from living your life to the fullest or to push you around while you simply put up with it. Decide today—with God's help—that you'll face fear head-on, overcome it, and do everything you can to live the life He has planned for you, free from fear.

Prayer: *Lord, when I feel fear, help me choose not to let it dictate my decisions or stop me from living the good life You want me to live.*

Blessings Instead
of Judgment

Do not judge, or you too will be judged.

Matthew 7:1

Sometimes when we feel insecure, rejected by others, or inferior to them, we struggle to simply admit we feel left out, ignored, or somehow less than the people around us. Instead, we become critical or judgmental toward them. But this is not the way God wants us to handle our emotions or to treat people.

We should choose to focus on God's love for us and to remember that He accepts us unconditionally (Ephesians 1:4–6). He calls us "the apple of His eye" (Deuteronomy 32:10) and says we are inscribed on the palm of His hand (Isaiah 49:16). The more secure we are in His love, the less we will feel critical or negative toward others. The greater our understanding of God's love for us, which we could never deserve, the more we realize that God loves everyone the same. He doesn't have favorites (Romans 2:11). If He loves people, we can choose to love them too and not judge them, with His help.

Notice in today's scripture that Jesus not only tells us not to judge people but also explains why we should refrain from doing so. It's for our own good. We aren't to judge others so we won't be judged. We do reap what we sow (Galatians 6:7), and if we sow criticism and judgment, we'll find people criticizing and judging us. But if we sow love and blessing into other people, we'll experience love and blessing too.

Next time you are tempted to criticize or judge someone for any reason, resist. Instead, choose to love and bless them.

———————

Prayer: *Lord, when I feel rejected or inferior to others, help me not to judge or criticize. Help me to love and bless everyone around me.*

How to Love Your Life

---

*So I hated life, because the work that is done under
the sun was grievous to me. All of it is meaningless,
a chasing after the wind. I hated all the things
I had toiled for under the sun, because I must
leave them to the one who comes after me.*

Ecclesiastes 2:17–18

Solomon, the writer of today's scripture passage, was so stressed out that he hated his life and ended up unfulfilled and bitter. These are not emotions anyone would choose.

So what's the secret to happiness and fulfillment in life? I believe it's making sure we obey God's will and give ourselves to what He has called us to do. This is not always easy. We sometimes struggle and grow weary along the way.

Let me encourage you today to think seriously about how you spend your time. As God leads you, cut activities and commitments out of your life until you no longer go through every day at a frantic pace and end up feeling stressed.

First, realize that you can't do everything. Then decide with God's help what you can do. This will make you more effective at what you're supposed to do and greatly increase the peace in your life. Peace equals power; without it, you'll stay frustrated and weak.

As you evaluate how you're spending your time, use this simple rule: If you have peace about it, keep doing it. If you don't have peace about it, stop. Feeling resentful or hearing yourself complain about it frequently indicates the need to make an adjustment.

God doesn't want you to end up like Solomon, hating your life and being bitter. His great desire is for you to love your life, enjoy being in His will, and be satisfied and at peace as you fulfill His purpose for you.

Prayer: *God, I believe You want me to enjoy my life. Help me make the decisions that will bring peace and fulfillment to me each day.*

DAY 20

Meditating Helps
Manage Emotions

Keep this Book of the Law always on your lips;
meditate on it day and night, so that you may be
careful to do everything written in it.
Then you will be prosperous and successful.

Joshua 1:8

One of the best ways to manage our emotions is to meditate on God's Word and let it help us with the way we feel. I love that God frequently tells us to meditate on—to ponder seriously—His Word, as though we are chewing on it in our minds like we chew our food in our mouths.

Recently when I meditated on several passages in the Bible, I realized that the Word has hidden treasures in it—powerful, life-giving secrets that God wants to reveal to us. They are there for those who meditate on, ponder, and contemplate His Word.

If we want a deep relationship with our heavenly Father, we find it by spending time with Him and in His Word on a regular, daily basis. This brings us an awareness of His presence in our lives and enables us to sense how His Holy Spirit wants us to live.

As we focus on God's Word, we will push away all desire to sin or to displease God in any way. We gain strength to deal with our emotions in healthy, godly ways. We learn to deal with anger and jealousy through forgiveness. We find courage to face our fears. We receive the comfort God offers us during seasons of sadness or loss. We can use God's Word to praise Him when we win the battles we face in life, and to express our joy and thanksgiving for all God does for us and for who He is.

Prayer: *Lord, help me discipline myself to meditate on Your Word and allow it to help me manage my emotions.*

Don't Let Your Emotions Lead You Astray

The heart is deceitful above all things
and beyond cure. Who can understand it?
Jeremiah 17:9

Today's scripture teaches us that our hearts are "deceitful above all things." Deception can occur when we believe something is not true even though it is, or when we believe something is true when it is not. We can easily fall into the enemy's trap of self-deception. The self always helps itself get whatever it wants. When we have a strong desire for something and our emotions are excited about it, we can easily deceive ourselves by telling ourselves whatever we want to hear. If my will wants something, my mind will give me a variety of reasons I should have it, and my emotions will certainly line up with what my will wants.

We must learn to live deeper than the shallowness of our own minds, wills, and emotions. Deeper living means we go beyond what we want, what we think, and how we feel and live by the Word of God. We must seek and humbly obey God's Word and His will, because that's where we find true blessings.

I encourage you to spend time regularly waiting in God's presence, asking Him to reveal any area of your life in which you may be deceived. Put your trust in God and in His Word, and follow the leading of His Spirit. Don't trust your own thoughts, desires, and emotions too much. Ask God for what you want, but be willing to change if you discover that it's not His will for you. He always does what is best for us. To avoid being deceived, we should be diligent to stay close to Him and His Word.

———————

Prayer: *Lord, help me to realize that my feelings can deceive me. Help me avoid deception and to trust Your Word and Your Spirit to lead me instead of my emotions.*

It's Okay to Be Angry— Just Don't Sin

"In your anger do not sin": Do not let the sun go down while you are still angry.

Ephesians 4:26

No one will ever reach a point in life where they don't experience a wide variety of feelings. One of those is anger. Being angry causes many people to feel guilt and condemnation because they have the false idea that Christians should not be angry but be peaceful all the time.

Yet the Bible doesn't teach that we are never to feel anger. It teaches that when we do get angry, we are not to sin. Rather, we are to manage or control our anger properly.

God gave me a revelation about this verse one time when I had been angry at my husband, Dave, as I was about to leave home to go preach. Guilt and condemnation whispered to me, *How can you go out and preach to others after getting so angry this morning?*

Of course, I was still angry, so even that question bothered me. But God caused me to understand that anger is just an emotion. Like all emotions, God gave it to us for a reason. Without the capacity to become angry, we would never know when someone mistreats us. We feel appropriate indignation when others suffer injustice. Without anger, we wouldn't be moved to act or take a stand against wrongdoing and evil. Anger, like pain, is there to warn us that something is wrong. This motivates us to try to make it right or improve the situation.

As with all emotions, Satan tries to use and abuse our anger and lead us into sin. But we have the power to resist him.

———————

Prayer: *Help me, God, when I feel angry, to handle it in a positive way so I will not sin.*

Feel Good about Yourself

---

*I praise you because I am fearfully
and wonderfully made.*

Psalm 139:14

How do you feel about yourself? Would you say you have a healthy self-image, appreciate your strengths, and love yourself, respect yourself, and think highly of yourself in an appropriate way? Or do you have low self-esteem, think too much about your weaknesses, devalue yourself in your mind or with your words, and struggle with self-acceptance? Many people focus too much on their weaknesses and allow them to negatively influence their self-image.

We all have weaknesses, but God says His "power is made perfect in weakness" (2 Corinthians 12:9). In other words, our weaknesses give God an opportunity to reveal Himself and work through us. For Him to flow through us, we must come face-to-face with our weaknesses and determine not to let them bother

us. We need to love and accept ourselves unconditionally—weaknesses, shortcomings, faults, and all—
because God loves and accepts us unconditionally.

I encourage you, when you feel unloved or unac-
cepted, to remind yourself that feelings are fickle.
Remember that God has created you in a unique way,
as a specially crafted person who is "fearfully and wonderfully made." He loves and accepts you fully and
has a wonderful plan for your life. Your weaknesses
and imperfections will not stop Him from fulfilling
His purpose for you or from working through you
to bless others. Tell yourself that God loves you and
that you will not allow your weaknesses to hinder you
from following Him wholeheartedly. Soon you will
have a whole new level of confidence and strength.

Prayer: *Father, thank You for the unique way You've made
me, with all my strengths and weaknesses. Help me to love
myself as You love me.*

Nobody's Perfect

He did not need any testimony about mankind,
for he knew what was in each person.

John 2:25

When Jesus' disciples disappointed Him, He was not devastated, because He already knew and fully understood human nature, as today's scripture teaches us. A major reason people get upset and disappointed in relationships is that they have unrealistic expectations of others. We should expect the best from people, but at the same time we should remember that they are human beings with imperfections, just as we are.

People tend to want perfection in others. They want the perfect spouse, perfect friend, perfect family, perfect neighbors, perfect coworkers, perfect pastor, and so on. But perfect people don't exist. Only Jesus is perfect. As long as we live in earthly bodies, we will manifest imperfection. God knows this, so His

Word teaches us how to handle people who irritate or disappoint us. Among other things, we are to be loving (John 13:34), forgiving (Luke 17:1–4), and kind (Ephesians 4:32), and we should bear patiently with people (Colossians 3:13).

People are not perfect, and expecting them to be without fault only leads to frustration. Instead, we need to have realistic expectations of others and set our minds to be patient and merciful toward them with God's help, as we would want them to be toward us.

It is important to expect good things to happen in your life while also knowing that no person and no situation is perfect. When we find ourselves growing frustrated with people, we should realize that our attitude in these trying situations greatly hinders our enjoyment of life. We can be realistic and still have a positive attitude as we deal with our own imperfections and those of the people around us.

———————————

Prayer: *Holy Spirit, help me not to set unrealistic expectations only to be disappointed. Help me to be realistic while also staying positive about myself and those around me.*

Trusting God When Emotions Are Intense

How long, Lord? Will you forget me forever? How long will you hide your face from me? How long must I wrestle with my thoughts and day after day have sorrow in my heart? How long will my enemy triumph over me? Look on me and answer, Lord my God. Give light to my eyes, or I will sleep in death, and my enemy will say, "I have overcome him," and my foes will rejoice when I fall. But I trust in your unfailing love; my heart rejoices in your salvation. I will sing the Lord's praise, for he has been good to me.

Psalm 13:1–6

If we paraphrased today's scripture passage in contemporary language, it might sound something like this: "God, I'm hurting so bad. I'm desperate for You. Have You forgotten me? How long will You wait before You do something for me? How much longer will my enemies seem to win? Look at what I'm going through. Help me, so my enemies won't overcome me and rejoice in my suffering. God, I trust in Your love, which never fails. I will rejoice and have a good attitude because of Your salvation and Your promises of love and mercy. I praise You, Lord, because You've been good to me. You are good all the time—even when I'm discouraged. I trust You and praise You in the midst of my troubles."

This psalm describes the principle we're focusing on in this devotional. We're learning that we don't have to deny that our emotions exist. They can be intense, but we don't have to let them control us. We can feel our feelings, but we don't have to follow them. We can't always change the way we feel, but we can choose what we do in every situation.

Prayer: *Help me, Lord, to pay attention to the way I feel and to make good choices as I deal with my emotions.*

Get Excited about God

And all the women who had ability and whose hearts
stirred them up in wisdom spun the goats' hair.

Exodus 35:26 AMPC

When people think about managing their emotions, they often think of dealing with anger, fear, or other negative feelings. But we can also manage our positive emotions, such as joy and enthusiasm. We can be excited about God and what He calls us to do.

In today's scripture, we read that the women who spun goats' hair were "stirred up," which describes their excitement. What were they stirred up about? Building the tabernacle, a portable sanctuary where the Israelites could worship God during their journey through the wilderness (Exodus 35).

Nothing on earth is worth getting excited about like God is. And there's nothing better in which to invest our enthusiasm and energy than the assignments He gives us. Paul encourages us in Romans 12:11: "Never lag in zeal and in earnest endeavor; be aglow and burning with the Spirit, serving the Lord" (AMPC).

A person doesn't have to be in full-time ministry to serve the Lord. You can serve Him as you love your family, as you're kind to people in the grocery store, or as you do your job with excellence and integrity. However and wherever you serve Him, be sure to do it joyfully.

If you find yourself lagging in zeal or enthusiasm, take time to stir yourself up by spending time in God's presence and thinking about how wonderful He is. Enthusiasm is contagious, so talk to a fellow believer—someone who is excited about God and serving Him with gladness—and let their joy influence you. God is awesome, and He is worth getting excited about!

_____

Prayer: *Thank You, God, for being so awesome. Help me stay joyful and enthusiastic about You and about what You've called me to do.*

Shake It Off

---

*And if any place will not welcome you or listen
to you, leave that place and shake the dust off
your feet as a testimony against them.*

Mark 6:11

Feeling rejected or unwanted is difficult and painful, but it happens to all of us at times. As part
of the human race, we have to realize that not everyone will always like us or accept us. When others
reject us, we have a choice to make: We can let it hurt
our feelings, make us feel bad about ourselves, and
wallow in it, or we can shake it off and not allow it to
bother us.

Today's scripture is an instruction Jesus gave His
disciples when He sent them to preach and minister
in various towns. Knowing they wouldn't be welcome
everywhere, He prepared them in advance to deal
with the rejection they'd face. In today's language,
He'd say to "shake it off!" He didn't want them to let

rejection upset them but to forget about it and keep moving forward.

Jesus' advice to His disciples years ago is exactly what we need to follow today. When people reject us, ignore us, exclude us, aren't pleased with us, don't like us, or don't accept us, we can shake it off and keep moving forward. We can do this because we are secure in God's total and unconditional love and acceptance.

When an insect lands on your arm, you simply shake it off. You don't keep thinking about it for hours, weeks, or years. But rejection can be so painful that we feel it for a very long time. Don't let that happen to you. Next time someone rejects you, shake it off!

Prayer: *When I feel rejected, Lord, help me shake it off, remembering that You love me and accept me unconditionally.*

God's Timing Is Perfect

---

*I will give you rain in due season, and the
land shall yield her increase and the trees
of the field yield their fruit.*

Leviticus 26:4 AMPC

In today's verse, God promises to send rain "in due season." We can learn a lot about managing certain emotions from this idea of "due season." It means that God has a specific time when He will meet our needs or release the blessings He has for us. His timing is not always our timing, and He doesn't always do things for us when we think He should. But He knows infinitely more than we do, and His timing is perfect.

When we understand that God has a due season for all things, we can effectively deal with emotions such as fear, frustration, and worry. We can relax, be patient, and trust Him to do exactly what we need Him to do when the time is right. We don't have to try to force anything to happen. We can just rest in God until it does.

Every person who walks with God has the opportunity and responsibility to surrender their will to His will, His purposes, and His plan. And God's timing is part of His will. Often, the unfolding of God's will takes time—sometimes much longer than we would like—and we must go through seasons of waiting.

Waiting is easier to endure when we make several good decisions about it. First, we choose to believe God's timing is perfect. Second, we determine to maintain a high level of faith and trust in Him. Third, we use our waiting time to serve Him and to do good to other people to the best of our ability. If you're waiting on something today, be encouraged. God will send it in due season.

Prayer: *Thank You, God, for Your perfect timing in my life. Help me to wait well.*

God Directs Our Steps

---

*A man's mind plans his way, but the Lord
directs his steps and makes them sure.*

Proverbs 16:9 AMPC

Today's scripture is one that has stabilized my emotions many times, along with Proverbs 20:24, which says: "A person's steps are directed by the Lord. How then can anyone understand their own way?"

I have been known to become frustrated when I'm in a hurry to get somewhere and find myself at a standstill in traffic. At first, I get a sinking feeling, then I become irritated. Then I say, "Well, since God directs my steps, I'll calm down and thank God that I am right where He wants me." I also remind myself that God may be saving me from an accident down the road by keeping me where I am. He always knows more than we do, and He can see everything. Trusting God is absolutely wonderful because it soothes our wild thoughts and emotions when things don't go as we have planned.

How do you react when you get frustrated or disappointed? How long does it take for you to make a transition? Do you act on God's Word or merely react emotionally to your circumstances? Do you let your environment control your mood, or do you let the Holy Spirit lead your response to what's going on around you?

Trusting God completely and believing that His plan for you is infinitely better than your own will prevent you from being frustrated when things don't go your way. It's impossible to be miffed at someone you really believe has your best interest in mind, and God always does.

Prayer: *God, I trust You completely, knowing that Your plans for me are infinitely better than mine and that You direct my steps.*

Give Yourself Good Fuel

The tongue has the power of life and death,
and those who love it will eat its fruit.

Proverbs 18:21

Have you ever noticed that what you say can influence what you think or direct how you feel? Our words can be fuel for our thoughts and emotions. They give our thoughts and emotions verbal expression. Feeling angry, fearful, or depressed isn't good for us, but verbalizing these negative emotions makes the situation even worse and affects us more than we realize.

Words are containers for power, and as such, they have a direct effect on our emotions. Words fuel good moods or bad moods. They also fuel our attitudes and have a huge impact on our lives and our relationships. Proverbs 15:23 says, "A person finds joy in giving an apt reply—and how good is a timely word!"

Today's scripture teaches us that "death and life are in the power of the tongue, and they who indulge in it shall eat the fruit of it [for death or life]" (AMPC). The message can't be any clearer. If we speak good, positive things that line up with God's Word, then we minister life to ourselves. We increase the emotion of joy. But if we speak negative words, then we minister death and misery to ourselves; we increase our sadness, and our mood plummets.

Why not help yourself first thing every day? Don't get up each morning and wait to see how you feel, and then rehearse every feeling with your words. This gives your emotions authority over you. Instead, take authority over your emotions with your words, and set yourself up for a great day.

———————

Prayer: *Lord, help me to help myself today by using my words to fuel a good mood and positive emotions.*

No Fear in Love

There is no fear in love. But perfect love drives out fear,
because fear has to do with punishment.
The one who fears is not made perfect in love.

1 John 4:18

We all feel tempted to fear at times, but we do not need to give in to this temptation, because God loves us perfectly and His love drives fear out of our lives. Because He loves us, He takes good care of us and helps us. We can rest in His love, confident and secure in the knowledge that it never wanes. He loves us all the time, in every situation.

When we realize we're allowing fear to rule us or influence our decisions, it signals that we need to grow spiritually and keep learning about and experiencing God's love for us.

The apostle Paul writes that nothing, no matter how bad it seems, can remove God's love from us or distance us from Him.

For I am convinced that neither death nor life, neither angels nor demons, neither the present nor the future, nor any powers, neither height nor depth, nor anything else in all creation, will be able to separate us from the love of God that is in Christ Jesus our Lord.

Romans 8:38–39

Notice the confidence that comes across in this passage. Paul says he is "convinced" that nothing can separate us from God's love. He says that nothing "in all creation" can drive a wedge between us and God's love. This includes whatever situation you're facing right now. You can trust and rest in the assurance of His love for you.

When you feel afraid, you can confront your fears by thinking about how much and how perfectly God loves you. This will make you strong, fearless, secure, and confident.

———————

Prayer: *Thank You, God, for loving me perfectly. Help me to remember that Your love casts out fear.*

Ask God about Your Feelings

---

*When I kept silence [before I confessed], my bones
wasted away through my groaning all the day long.*

Psalm 32:3 AMPC

Sometimes we feel more emotional than other times. This happens for various reasons. Maybe we didn't sleep well the night before, or we ate something that caused us to feel lethargic or grumpy. An occasional emotional day is not something to be too concerned about.

Sometimes though we feel emotional because something upset us the day before, and we didn't resolve it. We often suppress our feelings and pretend we don't have them instead of dealing with them. People who avoid confrontation often live with their souls full of unresolved issues, and these situations need closure before emotional wholeness will come.

I remember being unable to sleep one night, which is unusual for me. Finally, around five the next morning, I asked God what was wrong with me. Immediately I recalled being rude to someone the day before. Instead of apologizing to them and asking God to forgive me, I rushed on to the next thing I needed to do. Obviously, the Holy Spirit was dealing with me about my behavior. My conscious mind had buried it, but the mind of the Spirit wanted to bring it to the surface so I could deal with it. As soon as I asked God to forgive me and committed to apologize to the person, I was able to go to sleep.

If you feel unusually sad or like you're carrying a heavy burden you don't understand, ask God what's wrong. It's amazing what we can learn by simply asking Him for an answer and being willing to face any truth He might reveal about us or our behavior.

———————

Prayer: *Show me, Lord, anything I have done that is affecting my emotions in a negative way, and help me know how to resolve it.*

Emotions under Pressure

---

*But you, Lord Almighty, who judge righteously
and test the heart and mind, let me see your vengeance
on them, for to you I have committed my cause.*

Jeremiah 11:20

Today's scripture tells us that God tests our hearts (the seat of our emotions) and minds. When we want to test something, we put pressure on it to see if it will do what it says it will do—to see if it will hold up under the stress. God does the same with us. When we pray, asking Him to use us or to give us something or bless us in some way, His answer is often "Let Me try you out first. Let Me put you to the test." He wants to make sure we are strong enough to handle it.

Each day, we encounter many situations that are nothing more than tests. Sometimes they test our integrity, such as when a cashier gives us too much change and we need to decide whether or not we will do the right thing and give it back. And sometimes they test our emotions. For example, if we have to wait for a table in a restaurant and then we get a bad meal, it's a test. Will we feel frustrated, or will we stay calm? We may hope for an invitation to a certain gathering. If we don't get it, will we feel jealous of those who are invited, or will we simply find something else to do? In God's school, we don't flunk; we get to keep taking our tests again and again until we pass them. Next time you feel emotional pressure, tell yourself, "This is a test, and I want to pass it." Realize that God's tests always have a purpose and that they will ultimately lead to blessing.

Prayer: *Help me, Lord, to recognize the tests You give me and to respond to them as You would have me respond.*

Guilt-Free

Then I acknowledged my sin to you and did not cover up my iniquity. I said, "I will confess my transgressions to the Lord." And you forgave the guilt of my sin.

Psalm 32:5

Guilt is the sense of responsibility we feel when something painful or negative happens to us personally or when we've done something to hurt or cause difficulty for someone else. It is a feeling of regret over something we have done or perhaps something we failed to do. Guilt is a terrible feeling to bear, and we are not built to carry it inside of us. It affects our personalities, damages our souls, steals our peace, and dampens our joy. It can become like a prison without a door. Guilt leaves us feeling we somehow need to compensate for the wrong we committed or think we committed. The burden of guilt, combined with the feeling that we have to make up for what we have done or not done, leads to a difficult and unhappy life.

The good news of the gospel is that Jesus has paid for every sin we will ever commit and for every wrong we have done. According to Romans 8:1, there is no condemnation for those who are in Him. We don't ignore our sins. We confess them, as we read about in today's scripture. And when we acknowledge our sin to God and repent, He forgives us instantly. When the sin is gone, we have no reason to feel guilty. The feeling of guilt may not go away immediately, but we can say, "I am forgiven, and the guilt has been removed." When we make the decision to trust the forgiveness and the cleansing Jesus has purchased for us, our emotions will eventually catch up to our decision.

Prayer: *Thank You, Jesus, for paying the price necessary to forgive my sins and set me free from guilt. Today, I choose to walk in what You have provided for me.*

Be Confident in Christ

---

*For it is we who are the circumcision, we who serve
God by his Spirit, who boast in Christ Jesus,
and who put no confidence in the flesh—though
I myself have reasons for such confidence.*

Philippians 3:3-4

It is easy to put "no confidence in the flesh," meaning in ourselves, if we feel we have nothing to be confident about. But if we have many natural reasons for self-confidence, it is even more difficult to learn that putting our confidence in anyone other than Christ is foolish and a waste of time. It actually hinders our success instead of helping it.

God wants us to be totally dependent upon Him rather than being independent. In John 15:5, Jesus teaches that if we remain vitally connected to Him, we will have fruitful, productive lives in the ways that really matter. He also says that apart from Him, we can do nothing. All of our so-called success comes from our relationship with Him, so we have no reason to feel self-confident. We have every reason to be confident in God.

Jesus calls those who are weary and overburdened to come to Him and says He will give them rest for their souls (Matthew 11:28–29). This invitation is, I believe, especially applicable to all the self-reliant, self-confident people who are worn-out from trying to do things on their own. The apostle Paul, who wrote today's Scripture passage, could have felt self-confident about his Jewish pedigree and his many impressive accomplishments before he encountered Christ. But once he met Christ and experienced His grace, he realized that nothing he did had any value unless Jesus was first in his life at all times and in all things. What a great example for you and me to follow.

Prayer: *Jesus, help me remember that apart from You, I can do nothing, and that I must place my confidence in You alone.*

Walk in God's Favor

---

*Surely, Lord, you bless the righteous; you surround
them with your favor as with a shield.*

Psalm 5:12

There are days when we feel great about ourselves
and everything around us, confident that we
could conquer the world. Then there are days when
we feel defeated before we even get out of bed. We
must remember that feelings are fickle, but God's
truth is unchanging. One of the truths that will help
us find stability when our emotions are up and down
is the fact that God has given us favor. This means
He blesses us in ways we may not expect, He gives
us opportunities we may think we don't deserve or
haven't earned, and He makes things that should have
been difficult for us easy by His grace.

We know we have God's favor because today's
scripture says He surrounds the righteous with favor
"as with a shield." You may not always feel righteous,

but as a believer in Jesus, you are. He has made you righteous through His death on the cross, where He took your sins (past, present, and future) and provided cleansing and forgiveness.

Even though the Bible says we have God's favor, often we do not act as though we do. One reason we don't tap into God's blessings is that we don't believe we deserve them. Another reason is that we haven't been taught that God's blessings can be ours. Consequently, we haven't activated our faith in this area. So we wander through life, taking whatever the devil throws at us without ever resisting him and claiming what is rightfully ours.

Let's receive by faith the favor with which God has blessed us, expecting it everywhere we go, with everyone we meet.

———————

Prayer: *Thank You, Jesus, for making me righteous and for the favor of God that rests on my life. Help me believe it and receive it.*

Feel the Freedom

---

*Who is a God like you, who pardons sin
and forgives the transgression of the remnant
of his inheritance? You do not stay
angry forever but delight to show mercy.*

Micah 7:18

No human being is perfect. Everyone sins at times (Romans 3:23), and when we do, we often feel bad about ourselves. Sometimes we even think we can punish ourselves if we feel guilty enough about our sin. This is not true. Sin does have a high price, but Jesus has paid it in full. When He died on the cross, He provided forgiveness for all our sins—past, present, and future.

When we ask God's forgiveness for our sin, He forgives us immediately and even forgets our sins completely (Isaiah 43:25). He shows us mercy with no strings attached. Even if there are consequences of the sin, we can move forward free from guilt, regret, or shame because God's forgiveness cleanses us thoroughly, and His mercy gives us a fresh start.

For years, I was a rigid, legalistic person. I had never experienced mercy, so I did not know how to receive it from God or give it to others. Thankfully, God has helped me in this area. Now when I sin, I repent and receive God's mercy immediately. I do feel bad about the mistakes I make, and I am sorry for making them, but I refuse to live in bondage to guilt and condemnation.

Knowing that God has forgiven us and that His mercy is always available to us should empower us to resist negative emotions such as shame and guilt. Jesus came to give us a wonderful, abundant life, and God's forgiveness and mercy set us free to enjoy it.

Prayer: *Help me, God, to remember that You are merciful and to receive Your mercy and the freedom You offer me when I repent of my sins.*

Don't Let Reasoning Steal Your Peace

And they discussed it and reasoned with one another, It is because we have no bread.

Mark 8:16 AMPC

Today's scripture is part of a story in which Jesus' disciples did not understand something He said. When the Bible says they "reasoned with one another," it simply means they tried to figure out what He meant. To *reason*, in this sense, means to use natural, human effort to try to understand or figure out something. It steals our peace and keeps our minds and emotions in turmoil.

The disciples often became involved in reasoning when what they really needed was revelation from the Holy Spirit. He is able to give us the insight and understanding we need in any situation, no matter how confusing it may seem.

I was once addicted to reasoning. No matter what happened, I did not discipline my mind and spent too much time trying to figure it out. The Holy Spirit eventually helped me understand that as long as I was caught up in reasoning, I couldn't walk in discernment.

Discernment starts in the heart and enlightens the mind. It's spiritual, not natural. The Holy Spirit doesn't help us reason, but He does help us discern.

When we need to understand something, God certainly wants us to use the good minds He's given us and to employ common sense. But when our thoughts get tangled up and we lose our peace because we cannot figure something out, we have gone too far. At that point, we simply need to ask God for discernment, wait on Him to reveal what we need to know, and choose to be at peace.

———————

Prayer: *When I'm tempted to reason, Lord, help me stop, find peace, and renew my faith in You.*

DAY 39

How to Deal with a Downcast Soul

---

*Why, my soul, are you downcast? Why so
disturbed within me? Put your hope in God,
for I will yet praise him, my Savior and my God.*

Psalm 43:5

You may know that the soul is comprised of the mind, the will (ability to make choices), and the emotions. According to today's scripture, the soul can become downcast or discouraged and disturbed, just as it can be joyful and excited. When we are happy in our souls, we simply enjoy the happiness. But when we are not, we have to deal with our emotions.

Discouragement destroys hope. And without hope we give up. It also steals our joy, and the joy of the Lord is our strength (Nehemiah 8:10). In addition, it robs us of our peace, and God wants us to live in peace, not feeling anxious about anything (Philippians

4:6–7). So it's very important for us to learn how to manage discouragement when we feel it.

When discouragement tries to overtake you or when your soul feels disturbed, begin to break free from it by examining your thoughts. What you think about and allow to take root in your mind strongly affects your emotions. Think discouraging thoughts, and you'll get discouraged. When you change your mindset and begin to think positively, your emotions will improve.

Instead of thinking negatively, think more like this: *Well, things are going slowly, but, thank God, I'm making progress. I'm on the right path. I had a rough day yesterday, but today is a new day, and God is helping me.*

Practice this type of upbeat, positive, godly thinking, and you will defeat the discouragement and disturbances in your soul every time.

———

Prayer: *Thank You for loving me, Lord. Help me to think in ways that will encourage me, give me hope, and bring peace to my soul.*

Believe That Something Good Is Waiting for You

---

*"For I know the plans I have for you," declares
the Lord, "plans to prosper you and not to harm you,
plans to give you hope and a future."*

Jeremiah 29:11

Loss is part of life. Significant loss can be very emotional, and one reason for this is that loss is often permanent. While a painful loss may eventually be followed by something joyful and wonderful, the loss itself cannot be undone, and the emotions it brings must be dealt with.

Whether this involves the loss of a spouse, a friend or family member, a job, a home, or something else important to us, we must go through it. Drawing near to God through prayer and His Word is extremely helpful, and participating in support groups or seeking grief therapy may also be beneficial.

If you are dealing with loss today, I encourage you to face your grief, not run from it. Process it as God leads you to process it, and open your heart to hope, believing that something good is waiting for you on the other side of your loss. It may be a new relationship, the ability to help others through a situation similar to what you've been through, or a new job that is more fulfilling than your previous one.

When faced with loss, you have a choice, and you can decide that you will move forward. This decision won't eliminate the emotions you feel, but the emotions will subside as time passes and you begin to enjoy life again. If you are feeling stuck in grief and loss, that can change today as you choose to move forward with God's help.

———————

Prayer: *When I face losses in my life, Lord, help me turn to You for the help and strength to choose to move forward, believing something good awaits me in the future.*

DAY 41

Obeying When We Don't Feel Like It

---

*"Truly I tell you," Jesus replied, "no one who
has left home or brothers or sisters or mother
or father or children or fields for me and the gospel
will fail to receive a hundred times as much in this
present age: homes, brothers, sisters, mothers,
children and fields—along with persecutions—
and in the age to come eternal life."*

Mark 10:29-30

One of the emotions we need to manage at times is the feeling that we simply don't want to do something we know we should do. It may be inconvenient or uncomfortable, or we simply may not like it. In other words, we don't want to sacrifice. But many times, obeying God does require giving up something or doing what we'd rather not do. To follow His will for our lives, we have to come to terms with the fact that it often calls for some type of sacrifice and to be willing to do what He asks of us.

In today's Scripture passage, Jesus promises to reward those who sacrifice for Him. He says the rewards will come both on earth and in eternal life. Sometimes He asks for radical obedience, and radical obedience pays great dividends. It leads us to the personal joy and peace we experience when we know we are walking in God's will and to the other rewards He has promised. God is always aware of what we sacrifice, and He knows how to bless us in ways that make us glad we have obeyed Him.

Obeying God always brings a reward. It may not be exactly what we think it should be, but it is always what is best for us. It may not come when we think it should, but it will come right on time. I have found that God is a great rewarder. When we sacrifice in order to obey Him, He blesses us in amazing ways.

————————

Prayer: *Lord, help me be willing to give up whatever I need to in order to be obedient to You and experience the blessings You have for me.*

DAY 42

You Can Be Free
from Shame

I live in disgrace all day long,
and my face is covered with shame.
Psalm 44:15

Have you ever felt like the writer of today's scripture—as though you go through life wearing a cloak of shame? I felt this way for years, and I know it's a terrible way to feel. I also know there is hope!

Many people are "rooted" in shame. This means their shame is so deep that it functions as the root of a tree and actually produces "fruit" in the form of unhealthy thoughts and behaviors that negatively affect their lives and relationships. Shame is different from guilt, and it affects people more deeply than guilt. Normal guilt causes us to feel embarrassed, regretful, or bad about something we have done, while shame makes us feel bad about who we are.

When you and I make mistakes or commit sin, we feel bad until we repent and are forgiven. Then we're able to put it behind us and go on without any lasting harm. But when people are rooted in shame, it affects everything about their lives. They have such deep negative attitudes and feelings toward themselves that their negativity poisons everything they try to accomplish. They struggle more than people who don't deal with shame and seem doomed to failure because they have no confidence.

According to Hebrews 12:2, Jesus bore our shame for us on the cross. This includes both the shame anyone would feel in certain situations and the deeply rooted shame that affects some people. You don't have to live ashamed of who you are. Jesus has set you free.

Prayer: *Thank You, Jesus, for Your work on the cross and for making a way for me to live free from shame. Heal my heart, I pray.*

You Are Complete in Christ

---

*Jesus answered, "Even if I testify on my own behalf,
my testimony is valid, for I know where I came from
and where I am going. But you have no idea where
I come from or where I am going."*

John 8:14

Many people struggle emotionally because they simply do not know who they really are. They are not grounded in their true identity, and they feel lacking in certain ways.

Our identity is established as a result of who and what we choose to identify with. If we identify with people and what they say about us, we will end up in trouble, but if we identify with Jesus and His opinion of us, we will not have an identity crisis.

Today's scripture indicates that Jesus knew who He was because He knew where He came from and where He was going. Many of the Pharisees, the religious leaders of the day, were angry at Jesus' confidence in who He was. But no matter what people said about Jesus, He did not identify with it. He identified with what His heavenly Father said about Him. He identified with God.

Identification with Christ is a doctrinal foundation of the Christian faith. As a believer, you belong to God. Your identity is in Him, and you are complete in Him. This truth will give you confidence to walk through this world, dealing with all kinds of people, with your head held high. It will enable you to follow your heart and do what God leads you to do without becoming emotionally upset when people do not agree with you or your choices. The more firmly you are rooted in your identity in Christ, the more you will realize that you are not lacking in any way. You have—and are—everything in Him.

———————

Prayer: *Thank You, God, that my identity is in You. Help me grow deeper in the identity You give me.*

Finding Freedom from Emotional Pain

You have heard that it was said, "Love your neighbor and hate your enemy." But I tell you, love your enemies and pray for those who persecute you, that you may be children of your Father in heaven.

Matthew 5:43–45

Many of us have suffered emotional wounds over the course of our lives, or we may still be in emotional pain. These wounds can fester and cause us to struggle in various ways if we do not seek the healing God offers us.

Emotional wounds may come from abuse, rejection, abandonment, disappointment, criticism, judgment, or other types of hurt. If you have an emotional wound of any kind, I want you to know today that Jesus can heal you everywhere you hurt. According to the prophecy in Isaiah 61:1, Jesus came "to bind up the brokenhearted" and "to proclaim freedom for the captives." He heals our broken hearts and sets us free from pain and other forms of bondage. He also came "to comfort all who mourn" and to give us "a crown of beauty instead of ashes, the oil of joy instead of mourning, and a garment of praise instead of a spirit of despair" (Isaiah 61:2–3).

To begin to heal emotionally, we need to make godly choices while we are still hurting. Pressing through our feelings in this way can be difficult, but it's worth doing because it leads to freedom and wholeness. For example, according to today's scripture, the world would tell us to love people who are good to us and hate our enemies. But this leads to bitterness. And bitterness is a negative emotion that keeps our pain fresh and prohibits us from feeling peaceful.

Jesus says to forgive those who have hurt us and to love and pray for our enemies. This is the way to peace, healing, and freedom.

Prayer: *Thank You, Jesus, for teaching me to forgive so I can be healed and set free from emotional pain.*

The Lord Is with You

The Lord is with me; I will not be afraid.
What can mere mortals do to me?

Psalm 118:6

When the psalmist David wrote in today's scripture "I will not be afraid," I don't think he meant he didn't feel fear. I think he is declaring that when he did feel afraid, he did not let fear control him. Each of us should have that same attitude. In fact, it's the best possible attitude for a person to have. Fear is not from God, and we should resist it firmly in the power of the Holy Spirit. We may be aware of it, but we should not let it affect our decisions.

In Matthew 28:20, Jesus tells His disciples, "And surely I am with you always, to the very end of the age." This is not only a promise Jesus made to His disciples centuries ago; it is a vitally important promise from God for you and me today. There's no place you have ever been where God was not, and no place you'll ever be that God won't be there too. He is omnipresent, which means He is everywhere all the time. He sees everything, knows everything, and has all power. He is our Father, and we are His beloved children.

God wants us to know that we don't have to be afraid of anything or anyone, because He is with us. He is good and will take care of us. As David wrote, "What can mere mortals do to me?" People may try to intimidate you or frighten you, but they are mere mortals. God is all-powerful, and people are powerless compared to Him.

Prayer: *Help me, Lord, to remember always that because You are with me, I don't have to be afraid of anyone or anything.*

Find Rest in God's Presence

Repent, then, and turn to God, so that your sins may be wiped out, that times of refreshing may come from the Lord.

Acts 3:19

Sometimes life can be very emotional, and so much emotion can be exhausting. We may go through seasons of stress, seasons of sorrow and sadness, seasons of fear, seasons of confusion and uncertainty, seasons of jealousy and envy, seasons of tension and anger, and other intense, emotionally difficult periods of time. Especially when these emotional times are prolonged, we need to take a break. We need a little rest.

This rest is found in God's presence, in knowing He is with us no matter what we are going through. He is our refuge and our strength (Psalm 46:1). His

Holy Spirit is our Counselor (John 14:26), and He will help us know what to do in every situation so that we no longer feel stressed, confused, frightened, angry, jealous, or excessively sad. He may lead us to take a few days of physical rest or spend some time with a good friend. He may give us an idea that will help lighten our load in a practical way. He may even lead us to do something that will make us laugh. No matter how He leads us, the most important thing is that we stop what we're doing for a while and seek His presence. When we seek Him, we will find Him (Jeremiah 29:13). In His presence, burdens are lifted, peace fills our hearts, He restores our souls (Psalm 23:3), and we are able to rest. No matter what is going on in your life or how you feel about it, spend time today in God's presence and find rest.

Prayer: *When my emotions are intense, remind me, Lord, to find rest in Your presence.*

Dealing with Disappointment

Sustain me, my God, according to your promise,
and I will live; do not let my hopes be dashed.

Psalm 119:116

Disappointment often occurs when our hopes or plans are thwarted by something we cannot help or situations we cannot control. We can be disappointed by unpleasant circumstances or by people who let us down. We may feel disappointment with God when we've been expecting Him to do something and He doesn't. There are even times when we're disappointed in ourselves. No one gets everything they want all the time, so we need to learn how to deal with disappointment.

When we're disappointed, our emotions initially sink. Then they sometimes flare up in anger or a sense of injustice as we think, *This isn't fair!* As time goes by, and after we've thoroughly expressed our anger, our emotions may spiral downward again. We feel negative, discouraged, and depressed. The next time you're disappointed, pay attention to the activity of your emotions. But instead of letting them take the lead, decide that you will manage them. There's nothing unusual or wrong about initial feelings of disappointment. But what we do from that point forward makes all the difference in the world.

I learned long ago that with God on our side, even though we will experience disappointments in life, we can always get "reappointed." If we have a doctor's appointment and the doctor has to cancel because of an emergency, we simply make another appointment. Life can be that way too. Trusting that God has a good plan for us and that He orders our steps is the key to preventing disappointment from turning into despair.

———————

Prayer: *When I am disappointed, Lord, I choose to trust You, knowing that You have a good plan for my life and that You direct my steps.*

The Best Way to Feel about Yourself

Jesus replied: "'Love the Lord your God with all your heart and with all your soul and with all your mind.' This is the first and greatest commandment. And the second is like it: 'Love your neighbor as yourself.'"

Matthew 22:37–39

When a Pharisee asked Jesus what the greatest commandment in God's law was, He responded with the words of today's Scripture verses. What is most important for us as Christians is to love God, love people, and love ourselves. We often feel we do well in terms of loving God and loving others, but we struggle to love ourselves.

Part of loving ourselves involves *liking* ourselves and feeling good about who God made us to be. The best way to feel about ourselves is to feel positive, not negative, about who we are. If we don't like ourselves,

we will have a hard time liking other people and getting along with them. We may pretend to like ourselves, but pretense doesn't alter fact. Eventually, the
truth will come out.

To be everything God has created us to be and do
all He calls us to do, we need to have godly attitudes
toward other people and toward ourselves. We need
to be emotionally stable and rooted and grounded in
God's love for us (Ephesians 3:17).

When we are rooted and grounded in God's love,
we are secure in who we are. We can be relaxed and at
ease. We are confident that our worth as individuals
has nothing to do with our performance or anything
we do; it has everything to do with God's heart of
unconditional love and acceptance toward us. When
we begin to understand how God feels about us, not
only can we love ourselves, but we can also like and
enjoy ourselves.

Prayer: *Help me, Lord, to understand how You feel about
me so I can love, like, and enjoy myself.*

Follow God's Lead

He who watches the wind [waiting for all conditions
to be perfect] will not sow [seed], and he who looks
at the clouds will not reap [a harvest].

Ecclesiastes 11:4 AMP

Aren't you thankful that you and I don't have to be led by our emotions? We can be led by God's Spirit. All we need to do is be obedient to Him. When the Lord asks us to do something, any of us can be tempted to wait for a convenient season, a time when all conditions are perfect, as today's scripture mentions. Human nature causes us to hold back sometimes as we walk with God, wanting to wait until following Him won't be so difficult. Our emotions find all kinds of ways to delay doing what we know we should do.

I encourage you to be unafraid of facing challenges or taking on responsibilities, so that you won't procrastinate when God speaks. If you only do what is easy and what your emotions want to do, you will remain weak and shallow as a Christian. But as you meet resistance and overcome it, you will build your strength and grow in your faith.

God expects us to be responsible and take care of what He gives us. He wants us to use all He's given us to bear good fruit (John 15:16). If we do not use the gifts and talents He has given us when He directs us to, then we are not being responsible over what He has entrusted to us.

If you are a procrastinator, I urge you to heed the instruction of Ecclesiastes 11:4. You don't have to wait until everything seems perfect and your emotions are excited to obey God. Do what He says to do when He says to do it, and you will reap the blessings of obedience.

Prayer: *Help me, Lord, to follow You and to obey You promptly when You lead me to do something.*

Be Happy with What You Have

You shall not covet your neighbor's house.
You shall not covet your neighbor's wife,
or his male or female servant, his ox or donkey,
or anything that belongs to your neighbor.

Exodus 20:17

When you read today's scripture, you may think, "My neighbor doesn't have an ox or a donkey!" But the point of this verse, which is one of the Ten Commandments, is not as much about oxen or donkeys as it is about being happy with what we have instead of jealous of what others have.

Jealousy is a dangerous emotion. It makes us miserable on the inside and can do great damage to our relationships with the people around us. It can also have a negative impact on our health as well as on our relationship with God.

When we are jealous of others because of what

they own—their houses, cars, jewelry, clothes, or other possessions—it is usually because we are unhappy with what we have (or don't have). For example, someone who speaks badly of a person's nice new car—commenting that it's too expensive or that the owner must be frivolous or foolish—may really be saying, "I'm not happy with my car. I want your car." The same can happen with houses, clothes, and talents other people have as well as other areas of life.

Have you ever heard about a blessing someone else received and thought, *When is that going to happen to me?* Instead of being unhappy or jealous when God blesses someone with something you would like to have, you can train your mind and emotions to be happy for them. You can let their blessing be an encouragement to you, believing that what God did for someone else, He can also do for you.

Prayer: *Next time I am tempted to be jealous, Lord, remind me to be encouraged by the ways You bless other people, knowing that You will also bless me in the way that is best for me, according to Your perfect timing.*

Keep Your Love Warm

And because lawlessness will abound,
the love of many will grow cold.

Matthew 24:12 NKJV

Today's scripture comes from a passage in which Jesus is talking about signs of the end times. Some may be familiar to us, such as "wars and rumors of wars...famines, pestilences, and earthquakes" (Matthew 24:6–7 NKJV). But He also says that "the love of many will grow cold" (v. 12 NKJV) because of lawlessness and wickedness on earth.

The pressures of rampant evil, difficult circumstances, and frightening situations and the stress of living under such tumult produce an atmosphere charged with strife and trouble. This causes us to turn inward, trying to protect ourselves and solve the problems that affect us. It also makes it easy to allow ourselves to become hard-hearted and ignore Jesus' instruction to "Love one another. As I have loved you, so you must love one another" (John 13:34).

When love grows cold, negative emotions take over. We become angry, resentful, jealous, suspicious, fearful, and susceptible to other negative feelings. We become self-focused rather than focused on how we can help the people around us.

In many verses of Scripture, we read that we are to love other people. Loving one another is one way the world will know we are Christians (John 13:35).

In the midst of a wicked and stressful world, let's be sure to keep our love relationship with God strong. That will not only help us, but it will also empower us to keep our hearts tender and our love warm for others. When love is warm, we feel peace and joy, and we can share that peace and joy with others. This is what the world needs.

Prayer: *Lord, no matter what happens in the world around me, help me keep my heart from growing cold and help me stay stirred up in my love for others.*

DAY 52

Get Out of the Pit

---

*I waited patiently for the Lord; he turned to me
and heard my cry. He lifted me out of the slimy pit,
out of the mud and mire; he set my feet on a rock
and gave me a firm place to stand.*

Psalm 40:1-2

Anytime I read about a pit in Scripture, I think of the depths of depression. Throughout the psalms that David wrote, he referred to emotional lows as being in a pit. When he found himself in such circumstances, he always cried out to the Lord to rescue him and set his feet on solid, level ground. The Lord was faithful to help him.

Like David, nobody wants to be in the pit of depression. It is an emotionally difficult place that feels hopeless. When we are deeply depressed, we feel bad enough as it is. Then the devil brings thoughts of every negative thing imaginable to make the misery worse. He reminds us of our disappointments and tries to make us believe that nothing good will ever happen to us. His goal is to keep us so miserable and hopeless that we will not be able to cause him any problems or fulfill God's purpose for our lives.

According to Romans 14:17, God wants us to experience "righteousness, peace and joy in the Holy Spirit," so we know He does not want us stuck in depression. As today's scripture says, the pit of depression is a slimy place, and slimy places are difficult to climb out of without help. The Holy Spirit is our Helper (John 14:26 AMP). When we cry out to God, He pulls our emotions out of the pit, sets us on a rock, and gives us a firm place to stand so we can be emotionally stable.

Prayer: *Holy Spirit, when I feel like I'm in a pit, help me. Set my feet on a rock and give me a firm place to stand.*

Jesus Understands How You Feel

For we do not have a high priest who is unable to empathize with our weaknesses, but we have one who has been tempted in every way, just as we are—yet he did not sin.

Hebrews 4:15

Today's scripture speaks of our "high priest," and this refers to Jesus. He experienced every emotion and suffered every feeling you and I do, yet without sinning. Why didn't He sin? Because He didn't give in to ungodly feelings. He knew God's Word in every area of life because He spent years studying it before He began His ministry.

Luke 2:40 says that as a child, Jesus "grew and became strong; he was filled with wisdom, and the grace of God was on him." By the time He was twelve years old, He thought He was old enough to go to the temple in Jerusalem and be about His Father's business (Luke 2:41–52). But He still had years of learning before He entered His full-time ministry.

You and I will never be able to say no to our feelings if we don't have within us a strong knowledge of God's Word. Jesus felt the same feelings we feel, but He never sinned by giving in to them.

When I feel hurt, angry, or upset, it's such a comfort to me to be able to go to God and say, "Jesus, I'm so glad You understand what I'm feeling right now and that You don't condemn me for it. Help me, Lord, to manage my emotions and not feel condemned, thinking I shouldn't feel this way."

Because we're human, we have emotions. Sometimes they are intense. But we can be honest with God about them, knowing Jesus understands how we feel, and we can ask for and receive His help to manage them in a godly way.

Prayer: *Thank You, Jesus, for being willing to become human and to understand the emotions I feel. Help me manage my emotions in ways that please You.*

DAY 54

Be Slow to Anger

———————

Do not be eager in your heart to be angry,
for anger dwells in the heart of fools.
Ecclesiastes 7:9 AMP

Have you ever known someone of quick temper, whose default response to many situations was anger? I believe people who rush to anger lack the discipline of self-control. We can't develop into emotionally stable, mature, victorious Christians if we don't learn to exercise self-control by managing our emotions, especially the emotion of anger.

Ecclesiastes 7:9 is only one of many Bible verses about anger. Another is James 1:19–20: "Let everyone be quick to hear [be a careful, thoughtful listener], slow to speak [a speaker of carefully chosen words and], slow to anger [patient, reflective, forgiving]; for the [resentful, deep-seated] anger of man does not produce the righteousness of God [that standard of behavior which He requires from us]" (AMP).

Notice that the "anger of man does not produce" righteousness. Part of righteousness (being what God wants us to be) is fulfilling His purpose and plan for our lives and living up to our potential. We cannot do this without learning to restrain our anger.

We all want to fulfill our potential and do all God calls us to do, but we don't always want to operate within the boundaries of self-control. If we really want to grow spiritually, we must discipline our passions. This doesn't mean we have to be perfect or can never make mistakes. Although the Holy Spirit will give us power to control our emotions, we may still lose our temper at times. But as soon as we do, we should immediately confess it, repent, receive God's forgiveness, and move forward.

———————

Prayer: *When I feel angry, Lord, help me slow down and remember to ask You to help me control my emotions.*

One Day at a Time

---

*This is what the Lord has commanded: "Everyone is
to gather as much as they need. Take an omer for
each person you have in your tent."*

Exodus 16:16

Many people find it a challenge to manage their
emotions when it comes to thinking about the
future. So much about the future is uncertain, and
that can cause people to feel uneasy, anxious, or even
afraid. When we think about our unanswered ques-
tions and concerns about the future, we can find
comfort in the fact that God provided daily manna
for the Israelites to eat as they journeyed through the
wilderness.

God intentionally gave the Israelites just the right
amount of food each day (except on the Sabbath,
when He provided double on the previous day) and
told them to try not to hoard it or take more than they
needed. If they took more than they could use in their
households, it rotted and stunk (Exodus 16:20).

In giving the people only what they needed, God was training them to trust Him. By teaching them to rely on Him one day at a time, He was building their faith. Once they realized He'd send provision each day, they began to see Him as faithful and to know they could trust Him.

When we worry about tomorrow, we waste today. Maybe you're concerned about something in the future. Perhaps it's a specific situation like a big expense coming due, a doctor's appointment, or a move to a new city. Or maybe you just feel anxious about the future in general. Whatever it is, remember to take one day at a time, knowing that God will give you exactly what you need when you need it. It may not come early, but it won't be late.

———————

Prayer: *Help me, Lord, not to allow concerns about the future to make me anxious. Help me choose to trust You one day at a time.*

Want to Feel Fulfilled?

---

*Again, it will be like a man going on a journey,
who called his servants and entrusted his wealth to
them. To one he gave five bags of gold, to another
two bags, and to another one bag, each according
to his ability. Then he went on his journey.*

Matthew 25:14–15

Today's scripture is part of a story Jesus told about a man who was going on a journey and what he did for his servants before he left. Notice that he entrusted his resources to them "each according to his ability." It is important to realize that we don't all have the same abilities, skills, strengths, or talents. None of us can do everything well, but we can do to the best of our ability what God has gifted and called us to do.

Many people are frustrated and dissatisfied in life because they don't feel fulfilled. For various reasons, they are not doing all they know they should be doing, and they feel dissatisfied and discontent.

These emotions are not healthy, and they lead to other unhealthy emotions, such as resentment and jealousy toward the people who do feel fulfilled in life.

One of the servants in the story found in Matthew 25 hid his money in the ground because he was afraid. Similarly, sometimes we do not use the abilities God has given us because we are afraid. We may fear failure or loss or being criticized or misunderstood.

Don't be afraid or hesitant to take the abilities God has given you and use them for His glory. If you don't know how to begin or what to do, simply ask Him to help you. He wants you to "have and enjoy life, and have it in abundance [to the full, till it overflows]" (John 10:10 AMP), feeling satisfied and fulfilled each day.

Prayer: *Show me, Lord, what to do with the abilities You've given me, and lead me into fulfillment and satisfaction.*

Staying Happy in Relationships

Don't visit your neighbors too often,
or you will wear out your welcome.

Proverbs 25:17 NLT

When we think about our relationships, we realize they can have a great impact on our emotions. As today's scripture indicates, it is possible for us to wear out our welcome, meaning that others can reach the point where they wish we would just go home and give them some space. It is also possible for other people to wear out their welcome in our lives. To stay emotionally healthy, it is important for us to find a balance between giving and receiving in our relationships.

At one time in my life, I was learning to be content and trying not to want anything for myself. I continued to invest in the lives of several people who never gave back so much as a thank you or a word of encouragement to me. One day I realized that these relationships were draining and that I was enabling these people to continue in a selfish lifestyle. I prayed diligently and felt that God showed me that these relationships were unhealthy. In doing all the taking and no giving, these people were disrespecting the relationship and taking advantage of me. For me to have allowed this to continue would not have been good for them, so I had to set some healthy boundaries and learn how to avoid relationships that were exhausting.

We should choose our friends and associates wisely, looking for people who are there for us when we have needs, just as they expect us to be available for them when they need something.

———————

Prayer: *Lord, help me make good decisions about relationships so that both I and others can give and receive in healthy ways.*

Speak Well of Others

Brothers and sisters, do not slander one another.
Anyone who speaks against a brother or sister
or judges them speaks against the law and judges it.
When you judge the law, you are not keeping it,
but sitting in judgment on it.

James 4:11

People who feel insecure often judge and criticize others in order to feel better about themselves. In Matthew 7:1–2, Jesus warns us against judging others: "Do not judge, or you too will be judged. For in the same way you judge others, you will be judged, and with the measure you use, it will be measured to you."

The temptation to judge others is common. It's easier to find things to criticize about other people than things to affirm them. Some people immediately spot the one negative thing about a situation, no matter how many positive aspects there are. This is typical of human nature but not in agreement with God's Word. So when we are tempted to judge, we need to resist the devil and ask the Holy Spirit to help us stand against temptation and obey the Word.

In addition to what we read about judgment in today's scripture and in Matthew 7:1–2, the apostle Paul reminds us in Romans 14:10–13 that all of us will one day stand before God's judgment seat: "Therefore let us stop passing judgment on one another. *Instead, make up your mind not to put any stumbling block or obstacle in the way of a brother or sister*" (v. 13, italics mine).

Instead of judging other people, let's choose not to do anything that might cause them to stumble or pose a problem for them as they go through life. Let's help them or teach them by being a good example instead of criticizing them.

Prayer: *Help me, Lord, to affirm others and do good to them instead of judging them.*

Remember God's Faithfulness

You are my refuge and my shield;
I have put my hope in your word.

Psalm 119:114

Fear and anxiety can come against us for a variety of reasons, and sometimes we must fight hard to break free from them. The best way to do this is to seek help in God's Word. It has all the power we need and all the answers we seek.

More than thirty years ago, I was diagnosed with breast cancer. I was shocked because I had gone to the doctor for my regular checkup, which included a mammogram, and expected everything to be fine. When it wasn't, I became anxious and fearful.

One way God led me through this season was to impress upon my heart the need to stay positive and to make only positive comments based on His Word, such as "God loves me," "All things work together for good to those who love God and are called according to His purpose," "God is good," and "God, I trust You!"

I did this for about ten days before the surgery, and they were ten challenging days. Fear and worry would come, and I would purposefully call to mind that God had promised to take care of me. I would then declare the positive statements God had placed on my heart, and I could literally feel my emotions calming down.

In the end, the surgery was successful, and I've had clear mammograms ever since.

If you are struggling with fear today, look to God's Word and find peace. His Word has the power to bring peace to anxious emotions and to strengthen you in any situation.

———————

Prayer: *When I am anxious and afraid, Lord, strengthen me and give me peace through Your Word.*

DAY 60

Make Up Your Mind in Advance

The Lord is good, a strength and stronghold in the day of trouble; He knows [He recognizes, cares for, and understands fully] those who take refuge and trust in Him.

Nahum 1:7 AMP

Today's scripture speaks of "the day of trouble." All of us face times of trouble in our lives, and we are wise to decide ahead of time what we will do when they come. Let me encourage you to make up your mind to be emotionally stable before trouble ever comes. Ask God to help you in advance of difficulty, to keep you from excessive highs and lows, and to give you grace to remain calm and steadfast. Decide that you will stand in faith, remain thankful for what God is doing in your life, and trust Him, no matter what happens. When difficulties arise, keep praising Him, and don't ever give up or slide into an emotional pit.

We should not be surprised when we face difficulties. Jesus says that in the world we will have trouble (John 16:33), but we know that He will also strengthen us and enable us to do whatever we need to do in life (Philippians 4:13). God is our strength, our refuge, and, as today's verse states, our "stronghold in the day of trouble."

God knows those who trust Him, and He has a plan for our deliverance before our trouble ever starts. Romans 8:37 teaches us that we are more than conquerors through Christ, who loves us. And I believe one way to explain this verse is to say, "In Christ, we have won the battle before it ever begins." Therefore, we have no reason to be afraid of anything that comes our way. We can simply decide in advance that when trouble comes, we will stand strong in God and trust Him.

Prayer: *God, with Your help, I choose to make up my mind today that when trouble comes, I will remain emotionally stable, trusting in You.*

Don't Let Other People's Opinions Affect Your Emotions

Before I formed you in the womb I knew you [and approved of you as My chosen instrument], and before you were born I consecrated you [to Myself as My own]; I have appointed you as a prophet to the nations.

Jeremiah 1:5 AMP

In today's scripture, God tells Jeremiah that He knew him and approved of him before he was formed in his mother's womb. When God said He "knew" Jeremiah, He was not speaking of a casual acquaintance, but of the most intimate knowledge possible. God knows us the same way. He knows everything about us, even things we will never discover about ourselves. This knowing encompasses everything about us, whether we view it as positive or negative, as a strength or a weakness. He knows every mistake we will ever make—and He loves us and approves of us anyway.

God does not always approve of our behavior and choices, but He does approve of us. He clearly sees the difference between who we are and what we do. He loves our "who" even when our "do" isn't pleasing to Him. We all want other people to like us and approve of us. The way they feel about us often affects us emotionally. When they like us, we feel happy and good about ourselves. When they don't, we feel bad about ourselves. Our desire for approval can only be truly met by receiving God's acceptance and approval of us. It's important for us to strive to be God-pleasers, not people-pleasers. We tend to pay too much attention to how people respond to us, when instead we should be grateful that God knows us completely and approves of us unconditionally. We find our deepest security in Him and in what He thinks. As we walk in that, we can withstand the disapproval of other people and continue to love them in spite of it.

———————————

Prayer: *Lord, help me not to allow what other people think of me to affect my emotions. Help me seek to please You above all else.*

Help Is Here

---

*But the Helper, the Holy Spirit, whom
the Father will send in My name, He will
teach you all things, and bring to your
remembrance all things that I said to you.*

John 14:26 NKJV

You and I can make or break all sorts of habits
in our lives. We have physical habits, such as
exercise and getting enough sleep. We have financial
habits. We have social habits. And we have emotional
habits. Many times, habits are based in our emotions, but they manifest in other realms. For example,
emotional eating is a habit, and some people struggle with it greatly. When our emotions are intense—
perhaps we are sad, frustrated, or frightened—we turn
to food, typically "comfort food" rather than healthy,
nutritious food. The cycle of emotional eating can be
very difficult to break, and that can cause discouragement that leads to even more emotional eating.

When we try to break a habit such as emotional eating, we often find ourselves crying out to God, "Lord, help me, help me!" It is so wonderful to know that the Holy Spirit is always with us to help us all the time.

If you struggle with emotional eating, when you're tempted to overeat or to snack too much, you can pray silently, "Holy Spirit, help me not to overeat." In a restaurant where everybody at your table is ordering dessert, and you feel yourself start to waver, you can cry out in your heart, *Holy Spirit, help me, help me!*

I have found that if I depend on my own strength through sheer willpower or determination alone, I will fail every time. But if I am determined to resist temptation by calling on the power of the Holy Spirit, I find the strength I need to succeed—and you will too.

Prayer: *Thank You, Holy Spirit, for being my Helper. Help me break the habit of emotional eating and any other habits that are not good for me.*

God Heals in Every Way

---

*The Spirit of the Sovereign Lord is on me, because
the Lord has anointed me to proclaim good news
to the poor...to bind up the brokenhearted...
to proclaim the year of the Lord's favor...to comfort
all who mourn, and provide for those who grieve in
Zion—to bestow on them a crown of beauty instead
of ashes, the oil of joy instead of mourning, and
a garment of praise instead of a spirit of despair.*

Isaiah 61:1–3

God can heal us everywhere we hurt. When we think of healing, we often view it as physical. But God wants to heal us mentally, emotionally, and spiritually too. For a long time, I didn't know this, and my lack of knowledge caused me to live a dysfunctional life. Abuse and rejection had left me emotionally wounded until I discovered that God wants to give us "the oil of joy instead of mourning" and "a garment of praise instead of a spirit of despair" (Isaiah 61:3).

When we accept Jesus as Savior and Lord, a great exchange takes place in the spiritual realm. Our sin-filled, hopeless lives are swallowed up in His goodness, mercy, and grace. He gives us everything He has and is—and we are supposed to give Him not only everything we are but even what we are not. He takes our weakness and gives us His strength. He takes our sickness and gives us His health and healing. We give Him our sin, and He gives us His righteousness. He will give us joy instead of mourning, as long as we are willing to give up our sadness.

No matter what you have been through in the past or how much healing you may presently need, I believe it's time for you to enjoy God's favor. God wants you to enjoy yourself and your life. He wants to heal you spiritually, mentally, emotionally, physically, financially, and socially. I encourage you not to close off any part of your life to His healing touch. Invite Jesus into every area and ask Him to make you whole.

———————

Prayer: *God, I invite You today to heal me everywhere I hurt.*

The Cure for Insecurity

But God demonstrates his own love for us in this:
While we were still sinners, Christ died for us.

Romans 5:8

People who struggle with insecurity are self-focused and excessively concerned about what other people think of them. They cannot develop good relationships because they stay busy trying to impress other people instead of being good friends to them. Their insecurities cause them to be fearful, and their fears cause them to shrink back from opportunities that could add joy and fulfillment to their lives.

The cure for insecurity is receiving the love of God. It is like a healing ointment that heals the soul (inner life), and I think it's the only thing that can do that. Everybody wants to be loved, but we often look for love in the wrong places while ignoring God's love, which is being poured out on us all the time (Romans 5:5).

As Christians we may hear often that God loves us, but do we truly believe this? Do we understand the amazing power of His love? Reading or hearing a truth and processing it with our minds is much different from hearing with our hearts and actually believing and receiving it.

It's important to believe that God loves us because of who He is, not because of anything we have or haven't done. We cannot earn or deserve God's love. We know this because, according to today's scripture, He loved us enough to send His Son to die for us "while we were still sinners." When we believe this, insecurities are replaced with confidence—not in who we are or what we do, but in who God is and in what He has done to demonstrate His love for us.

Prayer: *Help me, Lord, to remember and focus on how much You love me, knowing that Your love heals my insecurities.*

God Is with You

Be strong and courageous. Do not
be afraid or terrified because of them,
for the Lord your God goes with you;
he will never leave you nor forsake you.

Deuteronomy 31:6

Like many people, I spent years trying to eliminate the feeling of fear in my life. I never saw it for what it was—a feeling or an emotion based on ungodly thinking. When I looked at my problems or potential problems, I saw them without seeing God.

Throughout Scripture, God said in several different ways, "Fear not, for I am with you." He said it to Joshua and to many others (Joshua 1:9; Isaiah 41:10; Mark 6:50; Revelation 1:17). The only reason I can find in God's Word for us not to fear is simply that God is with us. The name Immanuel, a name for Jesus, actually means "God with us" (Matthew 1:23).

No matter what happens in our lives, God is greater, and He is with us. We may not know what He will do to help us, or when He will do it, but knowing He is with us should be enough. He is for us, not against us. And if God is for us, it doesn't matter who is against us (Romans 8:31), because God is greater than anyone or anything (1 John 4:4).

I mistakenly thought that as long as I felt fear, I could not do what I wanted to do or felt I should do. I was wasting my life waiting for fear to go away. I prayed diligently for God to take away the fear, but that didn't happen. Instead of praying to be without fear, I should have been asking God to give me the courage to go forward in the presence of fear, knowing that He is always with me.

Prayer: *Thank You, Lord, that You are with me. Because You never leave me, I can move forward even when I feel afraid.*

Let Emotions Subside before You Decide

*He heals the brokenhearted
and binds up their wounds.*
Psalm 147:3

Many things happen to us over the course of our lives, and one of them is loss. The only thing I can think of that many people are happy to lose is weight. Other than that, loss can be devastating. We all experience various types of loss at some point, and it is an emotionally intense experience. It's also extremely stressful.

Sometimes loss is expected, and people have time to prepare for it. But this doesn't make the loss any easier to bear. Other times, loss is sudden, and an unexpected loss has its own complications. In either case, emotions are raw when loss occurs.

In the aftermath of any type of loss, we have

decisions to make. Some are major and will have significant impact. I often say, "Let emotions subside before you decide." This isn't always possible, but when it is, I encourage people to wait until emotions calm down before making big decisions. Emotions are fickle and unreliable. It's healthy for us to feel and process them, but it's not good for us to allow them to direct our decisions. I have heard many people talk about making emotional decisions, and I have made them myself—and came to regret them.

When we suffer loss, we must grieve in order to be emotionally healthy. Grief is a process that involves multiple stages and various emotions (see Elisabeth Kübler-Ross's books for more information on this). It's a good idea to allow ourselves time to grieve our losses appropriately before making important choices that will affect the future.

———————

Prayer: *God, help me remember not to make big decisions, if possible, when my emotions are raw.*

DAY 67

Let Yourself Cry

The hearts of the people cry out to the Lord.
You walls of Daughter Zion, let your tears flow
like a river day and night…pour out your heart
like water in the presence of the Lord.

Lamentations 2:18-19

One way we express intense emotion is through tears. Sometimes we cry happy tears, sometimes tears come from sadness, and sometimes we cry because we're frustrated or afraid. It's okay to cry. In fact, tears are good for us.

Respected biochemist William Frey conducted a fifteen-year study on tears. It revealed that tears shed for emotional reasons have a different chemical makeup than tears caused by irritants, such as chemicals or onions. Emotional tears contain toxins from the body that tears shed for other reasons do not contain. Frey and his team concluded that the chemicals built up in the body during times of stress are removed from the body in tears shed because of emotion. In addition, emotional tears contain high quantities of a hormone that indicates stress. Holding back emotional tears actually contributes to physical diseases that are aggravated by stress.

It's also interesting to note that only human beings produce tears as a result of emotion. Other animal species produce tears to lubricate their eyes, but only people cry because they are joyful, hurt, upset, or sad.

A friend whose beloved spouse died unexpectedly once told me that every time she wept over his death, she felt a palpable emotional and physical release. She also said that every time she allowed herself to weep, she told herself she was one good cry closer to healing.

The next time an emotion builds up in you to the point that you realize you need a good cry, go ahead and release the tears. They'll take you one step closer to healing.

Prayer: *Help me, Lord, to let myself cry when I need to, knowing that it's good for me and is part of the healing process.*

DAY 68

Know When to Keep Things to Yourself

---

*But Mary treasured up all these things
and pondered them in her heart.*

Luke 2:19

Mary was an ordinary girl who loved God when an angel of the Lord appeared and told her she would become the mother of the Son of God. Can you imagine everything she went through from the time the angel appeared to her until after the birth of Christ? I'm sure she felt a range of intense emotions.

Today's scripture appears near the end of Luke's account of Jesus' birth—after He was born, after the angel appeared in the sky, and after the shepherds visited Him. After all of this, what did Mary do? She still didn't talk about it; she pondered it in her heart. Whatever Mary thought or felt, she kept it to herself.

Sometimes, the best way to manage our emotions

is to be careful about what we say and to whom we say it. We can often stay calm about a situation if we keep it between ourselves and God. But if we tell certain people, they may be negative about it, and then we become negative. We may not be afraid of something, but when we talk about it, someone says something that suddenly causes us to fear. We may not be angry about a situation, but when we share it with someone, they convince us that we should be angry too. We may feel encouraged about a situation, but after hearing other people's response to it, we become discouraged.

Managing our mouth is part of managing our emotions. It's worth keeping some things to ourselves in certain situations so we can stay peaceful and positive.

Prayer: *Holy Spirit, give me wisdom as I talk about certain situations in my life. Help me not to share things when I don't need to and risk having my emotions affected negatively.*

A Peaceful Mind Leads to Peaceful Emotions

You will keep in perfect peace those whose minds are steadfast, because they trust in you.

Isaiah 26:3

Peace of mind precedes peace in every other area of our lives, especially in our emotions. Today's scripture promises perfect peace to those who keep their minds steadfast because of their trust in God. Perhaps you have experienced this. You have trusted in God completely in some situation in your life, and you have felt the peace that comes with the confidence that He will take care of you. Or maybe the opposite is true. You can remember a circumstance in which you could not seem to trust God, and it weighed on your mind, making you worried and fearful.

When we allow our minds to wander, overthinking the situations we're involved in and engaging in excessive reasoning (trying to figure out things), we push ourselves out of peace and into turmoil. When we think about the future and the problems that could arise or the responsibilities we will have, we can be overwhelmed. This kind of thinking is called anxiety. Likewise, we grow anxious and lose our peace when we spend today trying to figure out tomorrow or when we try to live tomorrow in our minds today.

We can only enjoy the peaceful, rich, and fruitful lives God intends for us when we learn to discipline our thoughts and resist anxiety by keeping our minds on God, steadfastly trusting in Him. As I say often: "Where the mind goes, the man follows." In other words, your thoughts are extremely powerful; they set the course for your life. Let your mind lead your emotions into peace today.

Prayer: *Lord, with Your help, I commit to keep my mind focused on You and to trust in You today so I will experience the peace You promise.*

DAY 70

Do You Feel Condemned or Convicted?

But he was pierced for our transgressions, he was crushed for our iniquities; the punishment that brought us peace was on him, and by his wounds we are healed.

Isaiah 53:5

Sometimes we feel bad about something we have done, and we are not sure whether we feel condemnation or the conviction of the Holy Spirit. Feelings of condemnation are not from God. He sent Jesus to die for us to pay the price for our sins. According to today's scripture and many other Bible passages, Jesus bore our sin and the guilty condemnation that accompanies sin. We should get rid of the sin and not keep the guilt. Once God breaks the yoke (or the power) of sin from us, He removes the guilt too. When we confess our sin to Him, He is faithful and just and forgives all of our sins and cleanses us from all unrighteousness (1 John 1:9).

How does condemnation differ from conviction? Let me explain conviction this way: We need forgiveness every day of our lives. When we sin, the Holy Spirit sets off the alarm, so to speak, in our conscience so we can recognize that we have sinned. He also gives us the power of the blood of Jesus to cleanse us from sin and keep us right before Him. This process is called "conviction," and it is of the Lord, while condemnation is from the enemy and only makes us feel miserable and guilty.

When we are convicted of sin, we may feel grouchy while God is dealing with us. Until we admit our sin, become ready to turn from it, and ask for forgiveness, we feel pressure on the inside, and it often brings out the worst in us. As soon as we come into agreement with God, our peace returns and our behavior improves.

———————

Prayer: *Thank You, God, for the conviction of the Holy Spirit. Help me always to repent and receive Your forgiveness when I feel convicted so I will be able to move forward in peace.*

DAY 71

Take a Lesson from the Farmers

Be patient, then, brothers and sisters, until the Lord's coming. See how the farmer waits for the land to yield its valuable crop, patiently waiting for the autumn and spring rains. You too, be patient and stand firm, because the Lord's coming is near.

James 5:7-8

Today's scripture about patience is written in the context of waiting patiently for Christ's return, but it applies to many areas of our lives.

Patience is not simply the ability to wait; it is the ability to keep a good attitude *while* we are waiting. Patience is also a fruit of the Holy Spirit that can be developed only under trial. This is why God allows us to go through challenges and trials instead of delivering us from them as quickly as we would like. He always has a plan to bring us through the difficult times we face, but He uses difficult times to help us grow so we will be stronger and have greater faith when the trial is over.

We can learn a lot about patience by thinking about farmers who wait for their harvests. The lesson here is that while we wait for something, we simply need to do what we know to do. That's how a farmer waits when expecting a crop. They water their seeds and pull the weeds—over and over again, day after day. Likewise, as we wait for God to bring something to pass for us, we keep doing what we know to do— pray, spend time in the Word, stand in faith, help and bless other people, and prepare ourselves as God leads us to receive the blessings we are waiting for. In addition, according to James 5:9, we don't complain. We simply trust God, knowing that He will do what He needs to do when the time is right.

———————

Prayer: *Help me, Lord, to wait patiently for You, doing what I know to do as I trust You to move in Your perfect timing.*

Highs and Lows

---

*Elijah was afraid and ran for his life. When he came to
Beersheba in Judah, he left his servant there, while he
himself went a day's journey into the wilderness.
He came to a broom bush, sat down under it and prayed
that he might die. "I have had enough, Lord," he said.
"Take my life; I am no better than my ancestors."*

1 Kings 19:3-4

After people experience an emotional high, they
often bottom out with an emotional low. One of
the most important lessons we need to learn as we manage our emotions is to deal with life's highs and lows.
This is what brings emotional stability to our lives.

We see this in the life of the Old Testament prophet
Elijah. One day he is at the height of his emotion—on
Mt. Carmel making a fool of the priests of Baal, calling down fire from heaven (1 Kings 18:30–40; 19:1–4).
The next day he is sitting in the desert asking God to let
him die because he feels so depressed. Maybe you can
relate.

When we experience an emotional high, we often

think, *Oh, if I could just feel this way forever!* But God knows we couldn't stand such intense emotion—even positive emotion—for too long. Too many emotional highs and lows can be exhausting emotionally, as well as mentally and physically.

As we continue reading in 1 Kings 19, we realize that the solution to Elijah's emotional low was simple and practical. He just needed to rest, recuperate, and eat a good meal.

When you go through emotional highs, don't be like Elijah and allow yourself to crash once you move beyond them. Don't become discouraged, get down on yourself, decide you are worthless, or complain about how happy you were yesterday but how miserable you feel today.

Simply say, "Lord, I'm feeling down right now, so I'm going to have to rest and build myself back up again. I'm going to spend time with You, Lord, and let You strengthen me."

———————

Prayer: *Help me, Lord, learn to balance life's emotional highs and lows and turn to You for help when intense emotions have worn me out.*

How Do You Want to Live?

But the fruit of the Spirit is love, joy, peace, patience,
kindness, goodness, faithfulness, gentleness,
self-control; against such things there is no law.
Galatians 5:22–23 ESV

When we are born again (2 Corinthians 5:17), we receive a new nature, which wants to follow and please God. But this doesn't replace our old sinful nature, which wants to indulge our selfish, self-centered, fleshly desires with the things of the world. The two natures exist side by side and are in conflict with each other. The strongest one always wins. In Galatians 5, Paul characterizes this as a battle between the works of the flesh (the old nature) and the fruit of the Holy Spirit (the new nature). The more you feed your spirit the Word of God, the stronger it will become, and vice versa.

Works of the flesh are listed in Galatians 5:19–21, and you can read about the fruit of the Spirit in today's scripture passage. When you consider the emotions involved in the works of the flesh and those produced as we walk in the Spirit, which way do you want to live?

I recommend focusing on walking in the Spirit rather than trying *not* to walk in the flesh. Paul says, "Walk by the Spirit, and you will not gratify the desires of the flesh" (Galatians 5:16).

I spent many years trying *not* to walk in the flesh. But I later realized that if I focused more on walking in the Spirit than on not walking in the flesh, there would be no room for the flesh. Only then did I begin to make progress. Hopefully this advice will help you cease striving to avoid the works of the flesh and empower you to live in the fruit of the Spirit.

———————

Prayer: *Help me, Lord, to abandon the works of the flesh by focusing on walking in the Spirit.*

DAY 74

Practice Patience

When the people saw that Moses was so long in coming down from the mountain, they gathered around Aaron and said, "Come, make us gods who will go before us. As for this fellow Moses who brought us up out of Egypt, we don't know what has happened to him."

Exodus 32:1

The Israelites mentioned in today's scripture didn't like waiting for Moses to come back to them after meeting with God. They became so impatient that they demanded something visible to worship. They refused to wait on God and ended up worshipping a useless golden calf that resulted from the work of their own hands.

Impatience is a negative feeling we need to avoid. It causes a lot of stress. The simple truth is that we all have to wait on things we desire, so we might as well learn to wait patiently. The fruit of patience is in us as children of God, but we have to use self-control for it to manifest (Galatians 5:22–23). The flesh is naturally impatient, but thankfully it can be controlled and retrained.

One of the best ways to be patient is to keep your mind focused on what you are currently doing. Don't be so focused on the destination that you fail to enjoy the journey. We live in a fast-paced society where everything moves quickly, and we can easily get caught up in the cycle of hurrying. But this is not good for us because it often puts us on edge emotionally. The slightest imposition or inconvenience can cause us to explode in frustration or anger.

Let's practice keeping our emotions calm and having a patient attitude with situations, people, and ourselves. Most of all, let's be patient with God when we are waiting on Him to do something we have asked Him to do. God has a perfect timing for all things, and He will not be rushed, so settle down and enjoy the wait.

—————————

Prayer: *God, I repent for the times I let feelings of impatience control my attitudes. Help me stay calm and patient as I wait on You and Your perfect timing.*

How to Avoid Frustration

---

*So he said to me, "This is the word of the Lord
to Zerubbabel: 'Not by might nor by power,
but by my Spirit,' says the Lord Almighty."*

Zechariah 4:6

Have you ever been frustrated because you were doing everything you knew to do in a situation, but nothing worked? I believe we all have. After years of being frustrated most of the time, I finally learned I was placing too much trust in myself and my own efforts and not enough in God.

As Christians, we often think we should be doing or achieving something. But if that were true, we would be called "achievers" instead of "believers." We are responsible for doing certain things, but many of us go far beyond our God-given responsibility and try to do things only God can do.

What needs to be accomplished in our lives won't happen in our own strength; it will be done by the

Spirit of God as we place our trust in Him. The Holy Spirit enables us to do what we need to do, and He does what we cannot do. We are partners with God; He has a part, and we have a part. Our part is to trust God and do whatever He leads us to do. His part is to work on our behalf and accomplish what needs to be done in our lives. God will not do our part, and we can't do His part. This is an important lesson to learn if we want to avoid frustration.

When I feel frustrated, I know I have slipped into trying to make things happen by my own efforts and stopped fully trusting God. As soon as I get my trust back where it belongs, which is in God and not in myself, I start to feel relaxed again.

———————

Prayer: *Lord, I commit to do my part, and I trust You to do what only You can do by Your Spirit.*

DAY 76

A New Way of Living

Therefore if anyone is in Christ [that is, grafted in, joined to Him by faith in Him as Savior], he is a new creature [reborn and renewed by the Holy Spirit]; the old things [the previous moral and spiritual condition] have passed away. Behold, new things have come [because spiritual awakening brings a new life].

2 Corinthians 5:17 AMP

According to today's scripture, when we place our faith in Jesus, the way we once were passes away, and we have all the equipment we need for a brand-new way of living. God gives us the ability to think and act in ways that please Him, and He offers to help us. But we aren't puppets, and He won't manipulate us. We must choose spirit over flesh and right over wrong. When we become new on the inside, we can choose to allow our renewed inner being to influence what we think, say, and do on the outside.

Biblical writers often use the term *the flesh* when

referring to a combination of the body, mind, emotions, and will. In Scripture, the word *carnal* often is used to describe people who live by the flesh, which some Christians do. Carnal Christians believe in God and have received Jesus as their Savior, but their lives appear to revolve largely around themselves, the desires of their flesh, and the impulses of their emotions. But feelings are often unreliable and untrustworthy when making decisions. It's nice to have feelings to support us when we make choices, but we can follow the leading of the Holy Spirit and obey God with or without the fuel of feelings. You may have a habit of following your feelings in order to stay happy and comfortable, but you can also form new habits. Develop the habit of enjoying good emotions without letting them influence your decisions in negative ways.

––––––––––––––––

Prayer: *Lord, when I need to make a decision, help me remember that I am a new creation and have the ability to follow Your Spirit and not my emotions.*

Keep Your Hopes Up

Let us hold unswervingly to the hope we profess,
for he who promised is faithful.
Hebrews 10:23

One way to manage the negative emotions of discouragement and despair, which we all feel at times, is to follow the advice of today's scripture and "hold unswervingly" to the hope we have in Christ. We hear the word *hope* often in secular settings, but godly hope has a different quality than worldly hope. Many times, when people say they hope something will or will not happen, they are vaguely hoping, but clearly doubting. They speak negatively about their circumstances and then wonder why things don't go well for them. True biblical hope is a solid foundation, a springboard for our faith to take off from and actually take hold of the promises of God. When we have godly hope, we speak and think positively, not negatively.

This may sound simple, but I believe real hope is a constant positive attitude that says *No matter what is happening currently, things will change for the better.* Satan cannot defeat a person who refuses to stop hoping in God. Hope is powerful. It opens the door for the impossible to become possible. All things are possible with God (Matthew 19:26), but we must cooperate with Him by staying hopeful and full of faith.

Being hopeless does no good. It only makes us unhappy, critical, and grouchy. Hopelessness leads to depression and many other problems. But because we belong to God and, as today's verse reminds us, He is faithful, we can choose to be hopeful in every situation. Be the kind of person who refuses to be negative, and believe things will get better.

Prayer: *God, I believe and declare that You are faithful, and I choose today to hope unswervingly in You.*

Making Wise Choices

I do not understand what I do. For what I want
to do I do not do, but what I hate I do.

Romans 7:15

Have you ever said or done something in a moment of intense emotion and then said, "I can't believe that I just behaved that way"? Have you ever felt shocked or perhaps embarrassed about your words or actions? We've all had this experience. Even the apostle Paul, who wrote today's scripture, struggled to do the things he knew he should do and not do the things he shouldn't.

Without God's help we have difficulty doing things in moderation. We may eat too much, spend too much, entertain ourselves too much, or say too much. When we give in to excess, we feel like doing something so we do it, giving no thought to the consequences. Later, we regret it.

We don't have to live in regret. The Holy Spirit

enables us to make wise choices. He urges us, guides us, and leads us, but we still have to cast the deciding vote. If you have been casting an unhealthy or foolish vote, all you need to do is change it. Make a decision not to do what you feel like doing unless it agrees with God's will.

Wise choices have nothing to do with feelings. You do not have to feel a certain way to choose to make good decisions. Making wise choices isn't always easy, but it is much better than suffering the consequences of a foolish decision. Even when something is not easy, through Christ we can choose to have a positive attitude because we know we are using wisdom in our lives.

Prayer: *Help me, God, to follow Your Holy Spirit and make wise choices.*

Fear Has No Power
over You

---

*Have I not commanded you? Be strong
and courageous. Do not be afraid;
do not be discouraged, for the Lord your God
will be with you wherever you go.*

Joshua 1:9

God called Joshua to lead the people of Israel into the Promised Land. This was a big job, and before sending him out to do it, He told him not to be afraid. For us to understand what God was really saying to Joshua, we need to understand the meaning of the word *fear*.

Over the years I've studied a lot about fear. To *fear* means "to take flight" or "to run from." It's also defined as an unpleasant emotion caused by the belief (thought) of harm or pain. A full definition of *fear* involves more than these ideas, but let's focus today on the fact that to fear is to run away from something due to an unpleasant emotion or feeling that we may suffer or be harmed.

If we view fear as running away from something, we can see that God was not telling Joshua not to *feel* fear. Instead, He was warning him that he would feel fear, and that when he felt afraid, he was not to flee because He (God) would be with him.

Understanding that we can feel fear and move forward anyway has been life-changing for me and for many other people. We do not need to wait for feelings of fear to go away, because they may never disappear. But we can do what we want to do or feel God wants us to do even if we feel afraid. Because of this, fear has no power over us.

––––––––––

Prayer: *Lord, help me understand fear so I can move forward and live in victory over it even when I feel afraid.*

Roots and Fruits

Each tree is recognized by its own fruit.
People do not pick figs from thornbushes,
or grapes from briers.

Luke 6:44

Trees are known and identified by their fruit, and people are much the same way. If you could look at the roots of the life of a person who is emotionally unhealthy, you would see that they lead to things like rejection, abuse, guilt, jealousy, shame, and other negative thoughts and feelings.

If you have recognized unhealthy attitudes in yourself, they are most likely the bitter fruit of something rooted in your thinking. They may have come from unhealthy or traumatic experiences during childhood or from being exposed to bad examples in your early years. If parents, teachers, or other authority figures told you during your youth that you were no good, that there was something wrong with you, that you couldn't do anything right, and that you were worthless and would never amount to anything, you might actually believe it.

Research has shown that when people believe something about themselves strongly enough, they actually begin to behave the way they perceive themselves. They will think, feel, and act according to what they have experienced or been told.

But I have good news: Your mind can be renewed by God's Word (Romans 12:2). This does not happen immediately or even quickly. It may take a while, but it is possible with the help of the Holy Spirit, and it is worth the time it takes.

God wants you to bear good fruit, and He will help you do so by replacing unhealthy roots with strong, healthy roots in your thoughts, emotions, and actions as you meditate on His Word.

Prayer: *God, as I meditate on Your Word, help me replace roots that lead to unhealthy thinking, feelings, and behaviors with ones that lead to healthy thoughts, emotions, and actions.*

No Shame

Do not be afraid; you will not be put to shame.
Do not fear disgrace; you will not be humiliated.
You will forget the shame of your youth and remember
no more the reproach of your widowhood.

Isaiah 54:4

Shame is a condition that affects our emotions in powerful ways. It can cause us to feel embarrassed about who we are and inferior to other people. It can make us fearful for others to know us as we truly are, and it can hinder our ability to engage in intimate relationships. Thankfully, God can heal us from the shame we have experienced and from the emotional impact it has had on us.

According to today's scripture, the Lord promises to remove shame and dishonor from us to the point that we will forget it. In fact, God has promised that in their place He will pour out upon us a double portion of blessing. We will possess double what we have lost, and we will have everlasting joy (Isaiah 61:7).

If you struggle with shame, ask the Lord to work a healing miracle in your mind and emotions. Let Him come in and fulfill what He came to do: heal your broken heart, bind up your wounds, proclaim your freedom, give you joy in place of mourning, and clothe you with a garment of praise instead of "a disheartened spirit," so you will be called a tree of righteousness, strong and magnificent, and in right standing with God (Isaiah 61:1–3 AMP).

As God heals you, your spiritual roots will go deep in the love of Christ, who, by His sacrifice on the cross, has broken the power of sin and guilt, cleansed you, healed you, forgiven you, and set you free to live a new life of health and wholeness. When you find your life in Him, you have no shame.

Prayer: *Thank You, God, for completely setting me free from shame and the way it has affected me emotionally. Help me always to remember that there is no shame in You.*

Hold Your Head Up

But you, Lord, are a shield around me,
my glory, the One who lifts my head high.
Psalm 3:3

In Psalm 3:1–2, the psalmist writes about his distressing situation. But in today's scripture, he declares his confidence in the Lord, the One who lifts his head.

When we are depressed and discouraged, everything around us seems hopeless. Sometimes this feeling affects us physically. We lack energy and lose strength; our heads and hands hang down, just as our hearts feel down. Even our voices are lowered. We become downcast because we focus on our problems rather than on the Lord. We may be tempted to say "Oh, what's the use?" and give up.

No matter what makes us feel downcast, the Lord encourages us throughout His Word to lift our heads and our hands and look to Him (Genesis 13:14; Psalm 24:7; 1 Timothy 2:8).

When people disappoint us or when situations threaten to overwhelm or defeat us, instead of becoming discouraged and depressed, God wants us to look at the possibilities, not the problems around us, trusting Him to lead us into an even better situation—because He has one for us. He encourages us to look at Him because He has plans to bless and increase us abundantly.

Whatever you are facing today, you have only two options: quit or keep going. If you decide to keep going, again you have only two choices: hang your head in depression and misery or lift your head high in hope and joy. Although there are downers in this life, there are also lifters. Choose to focus on the lifters today.

Prayer: *Lord, when I feel downcast, help me look to You as the lifter of my head and focus on Your promises instead of my problems.*

Pitiful or Powerful?

Then Jesus said to him, "Get up!
Pick up your mat and walk."

John 5:8

In John 5:1–9, we read about a man who had been lying beside a pool for thirty-eight years, waiting to be healed. He was not only sick physically, but he was also sick in his soul. Sicknesses of the soul can be harder to deal with than sicknesses of the body. I believe the condition of his body and soul stole his confidence and caused him to give up gradually, to the point that he was filled with self-pity.

In John 5:6–7, when Jesus asked the man if he wanted to get well, he said he had no one to help him get into the pool where he could be healed. Jesus did not stand there and pity the man. Instead, He told him to get up and walk. He had compassion on him, but He did not feel sorry for him or pity him because He knew it would not help him. Jesus was not being harsh in telling the man to get up and walk. He was trying to set him free.

Self-pity is a major problem. I know, because I lived in it for many years. God finally helped me understand that I could be pitiful or I could be powerful, but I could not be both. If I wanted to be powerful, I had to give up self-pity.

Like the man in John 5, Jesus did not give me pity either. His refusal to let me wallow in self-pity was a turning point in my life. If you will reject self-pity, actively look to God, and do what He instructs you to do, He will set you free.

———————

Prayer: *Lord, help me resist the temptation to feel self-pity. Instead, help me look to You to show me the way to healing and freedom.*

Tell God How You Feel

My bones suffer mortal agony as my foes taunt me,
saying to me all day long, "Where is your God?"
Why, my soul, are you downcast? Why so disturbed
within me? Put your hope in God, for I will
yet praise him, my Savior and my God.

Psalm 42:10–11

One reason we can relate to the psalms that David wrote is that he did not hesitate to tell God exactly how he felt. No matter how discouraged or fearful he was at times, he was open with God and always trusted Him to be faithful to him. He was also determined to praise God regardless of his circumstances.

I believe it was emotionally healthy for David to express to God how he really felt. It was a way of releasing his negative feelings so they couldn't harm his inner being while he was waiting for God's deliverance. David frequently told God how he felt or what his circumstances were and then said something like, "*But* I will trust God. I will praise God, who helps me."

I would never suggest that you stuff your feelings inside and not express them. That wouldn't be healthy. My purpose is not to encourage you to pretend everything is fine while you feel anger, sadness, or some other emotion. People who repress pain and never learn to deal with it properly eventually either explode or implode. Neither is a good choice. We don't want to deny the existence of emotions, but we can deny them the right to rule over us.

Instead, follow David's example and express yourself honestly to God or to a person you trust whom God wants to use. To express yourself in a godly way, always remember to put your hope in God—to praise Him and speak of His goodness and unfailing love.

Prayer: *Thank You, Lord, for listening to me when I express my feelings. No matter how I feel, help me always to remember Your love and to praise You.*

No Competition

A dispute also arose among them as to which
of them was considered to be greatest. Jesus said
to them, "The kings of the Gentiles lord it
over them; and those who exercise authority
over them call themselves Benefactors."

Luke 22:24-25

Early in my life, I struggled with jealousy and envy. This is common among insecure people. If we are not secure about our worth and value as unique individuals, we will compare ourselves to other people and compete with anyone who appears to be successful, smart, attractive, or doing well in other ways.

One of God's best gifts to me is that He has taught me that I am an individual with a God-ordained, unique, personal plan for my life. This has given me great joy and freedom, as I now live with the assurance that I don't need to compete with or compare myself to anyone.

I am always encouraged that there is hope for me when I realize that the disciples wrestled with many of the same things you and I do. In today's Scripture passage, Jesus was talking to some of His disciples as they argued about who was the "greatest." He responded to them by saying that the greatest was actually the one willing to be a servant (Luke 22:26 AMP). In other words, He says that greatness is humility.

When we feel insecure, we view ourselves as "less than" other people. But when we are humble before God, we realize that He has made us as unique individuals, loves us unconditionally, and values us so much that He sent His Son to die for our sins so we could live in relationship with Him. And we realize we have no need to compete with anyone else.

Prayer: *Help me, Lord, to see myself as You see me—precious, unique, and valuable. Help me break free from insecurity and walk in humility before You and others.*

Hopeful Expectation

But those who hope in the Lord will renew
their strength. They will soar on wings
like eagles; they will run and not grow weary,
they will walk and not be faint.

Isaiah 40:31

Today's scripture is a well-known verse about waiting on the Lord. We may think this means waiting on God in terms of allowing time to pass while we trust Him to move in our lives in a certain way, perhaps as an answer to prayer or to fulfill a promise in His Word. But the Amplified Bible, Classic Edition of the first part of this verse gives us important insight into what it really means: "But those who wait for the Lord [who expect, look for, and hope in Him]" (italics mine). When we understand waiting this way, we see that it is active, not passive.

To wait on God is to expect and trust Him to do what we need Him to do, to look for Him to work in a situation, and to hope in Him. This kind of waiting leads us to spend time with Him in His Word and in His presence. We don't worry while we wait on God; we don't get frustrated or upset while we wait on God. We don't question or try to figure things out in our minds, allowing our thoughts to go places they don't need to go. We rest. And we go about our lives with a sense of hopeful expectation.

Being able to wait with hopeful expectation is a sign of spiritual maturity. When we do have to wait on something, we can relax in God's presence. As we wait on Him, our strength is renewed, as today's scripture promises.

Prayer: *Lord, help me to wait actively, not passively, with hopeful expectation as I look for You to work in my life.*

How Do You Feel about Yourself?

For we are His workmanship, created in Christ Jesus for good works, which God prepared beforehand that we should walk in them.

Ephesians 2:10 NKJV

When we think of managing our emotions, we usually think about how we feel about a situation or another person. We don't often think about managing the way we feel about ourselves. But we all have a relationship with ourselves, and we have certain ways we feel about who we are. We may be happy with ourselves, but we may also be angry with ourselves or ashamed of ourselves at times. We may feel frustrated about certain aspects of our personality, our appearance, or our abilities. Some people feel undesirable, while others feel they are wonderful. Our emotions about ourselves can be varied and fickle, just as our feelings about circumstances or other people can change.

The way we feel about ourselves influences what we can accomplish in life. This is one reason that growing in emotional stability is so important. If we feel courageous and strong, we approach things with confidence. If we feel negative, we have low expectations of ourselves, and we tend to meet them.

If you feel bad about yourself, let me encourage you today. First, remember today's scripture and realize that God has a plan for your life. He's designed that plan especially for you and created you to succeed in it. Second, remember that you are "fearfully and wonderfully made" (Psalm 139:14). God has made you special and unique. Third, remember that, according to Philippians 4:13, you can do all things through Christ, who strengthens you. Let these truths lead you to feel great about yourself and to be confident that you can do whatever God calls you to do.

————————

Prayer: *Thank You, Lord, for creating me just the way You want me to be. Help me to feel good about myself and confident that I can do everything I need to do through Christ, who gives me strength.*

DAY 88

Use Your Mouth to Boost Your Mood

Do everything without grumbling or arguing, so that you may become blameless and pure, "children of God without fault in a warped and crooked generation." Then you will shine among them like stars in the sky.

Philippians 2:14–15

In today's Scripture passage, Paul instructs us to do all things without complaining or arguing. In the Amplified Bible, Classic Edition, verse 14 states that we are to "do all things without grumbling and fault-finding and complaining [against God] and questioning and doubting" among ourselves.

When you have a bad day or encounter trials and difficulties, you have a choice to make. You can grumble, complain, and feel resentful, or you can decide to remain joyful and peaceful, speaking words of praise and worship to God. Anyone can be grumpy and complain when they don't like their circumstances, but as followers of Christ, we are called to live differently. We are called to be overcomers, and part of overcoming is maintaining a good attitude and using our words to speak positively when everything is not as we would like it to be.

If the people around us know we are Christians, yet we murmur and complain like everyone else, we weaken our witness to them, and we don't shine the light of God's love to them, as today's scripture mentions. To be good witnesses, we need to resist the temptation to complain. Can you get through one day without complaining about anything? Can I? I admit that I have not arrived at the place of perfection yet, but I have made progress over the years and will keep pressing toward God's will.

You and I can use our words to boost our moods. Even if we feel cranky, if we refuse to complain and instead begin to speak positive, uplifting words, we'll find ourselves feeling better soon.

Prayer: *Lord, help me to use my mouth to speak positively instead of complaining.*

It's Always Time to Praise God

---

*I will bless the Lord at all times; His praise
shall continually be in my mouth.*

Psalm 34:1 AMP

If you are like most Christians, you have days when
you feel you don't have enough words to praise
God sufficiently. Other days you may not be able to
think of a single reason to praise Him because you
feel frustrated or discouraged. This happens because
of emotional highs and lows. But notice that David
says in today's scripture that he will bless the Lord "at
all times." He doesn't say he'll praise God only when
it's convenient or when it feels good and everything is
going his way. And he doesn't say he will not praise
God when he doesn't feel like it.

God is worthy of our praise at all times because
of who He is and because of all He has done for us.

He deserves our praise, worship, and thanksgiving in every situation, whether we think the circumstance is positive or negative. Mature Christians understand this and live a life of praise to God, regardless of how they feel about what's happening in their lives at the time.

We all feel tempted to erupt in anger or to sulk at times. We all feel paralyzed by fear or tormented by jealousy and envy. But we can manage these emotions and decide to praise God in spite of them. Praise is powerful—powerful enough to soothe raw emotions, calm frightened feelings, and lift us out of despair. God is worthy of our praise all the time, and He enjoys it. But it doesn't change Him; it changes us.

———————

Prayer: *Lord, help me to remember that praise is powerful and to choose to praise You even when I feel like sulking or being angry because of my circumstances.*

Rejoice in the Lord!

Rejoice in the Lord always.
I will say it again: Rejoice!
Philippians 4:4

Paul's letter to the Philippians has been called "an epistle of joy," and Paul mentions joy frequently in it. Notice that in today's scripture, Paul encourages his readers to rejoice *"in the Lord"* (italics mine). This tells us that we are to rejoice in God always. We cannot always rejoice in our circumstances or in the conditions in which we sometimes find ourselves, but we can rejoice in the Lord at all times. Paul suffered greatly at various points throughout his life, so he understood that while joy is an emotion, it is also a choice. Even when we don't feel happy, we can choose to find joy in God.

How do we rejoice in the Lord? We start by thinking about what we have in Christ, rather than about what we don't have in life. For example, we are forgiven of all of our sins, our names are written in the Lamb's Book of Life, and we will live in God's presence eternally. No matter what we don't have, we always have hope, and hope is powerful. We also have God's unconditional love, His complete acceptance, His strength, His guidance, His peace, His grace, and other wonderful blessings that are too many to count.

I encourage you to choose to think about what you *do have* rather than what you don't have, and you'll find your level of joy rising. Our thinking is the foundation of our emotions, and if we want to have pleasant emotions such as joy, we need to set our minds on things that produce them.

Prayer: *Lord, today I choose to focus on what I do have, not what I don't have, and to rejoice in You at all times.*

Do you have a real relationship with Jesus?

God loves you! He created you to be a special, unique, one-of-a-kind individual, and He has a specific purpose and plan for your life. And through a personal relationship with your Creator—God—you can discover a way of life that will truly satisfy your soul.

No matter who you are, what you've done, or where you are in your life right now, God's love and grace are greater than your sin—your mistakes. Jesus willingly gave His life so you can receive forgiveness from God and have new life in Him. He's just waiting for you to invite Him to be your Savior and Lord.

If you are ready to commit your life to Jesus and follow Him, all you have to do is ask Him to forgive your sins and give you a fresh start in the life you are meant to live. Begin by praying this prayer . . .

Lord Jesus, thank You for giving Your life
for me and forgiving me of my sins so I can have
a personal relationship with You. I am sincerely
sorry for the mistakes I've made, and I know
I need You to help me live right.

Your Word says in Romans 10:9, "If you declare with your mouth, 'Jesus is Lord,' and believe in your heart that God raised him from the dead, you will be saved" (NIV). I believe You are the Son of God and confess You as my Savior and Lord. Take me just as I am, and work in my heart, making me the person You want me to be. I want to live for You, Jesus, and I am so grateful that You are giving me a fresh start in my new life with You today. I love You, Jesus!

It's so amazing to know that God loves us so much! He wants to have a deep, intimate relationship with us that grows every day as we spend time with Him in prayer and Bible study. And we want to encourage you in your new life in Christ.

Please visit joycemeyer.org/salvation to request Joyce's book *A New Way of Living*, which is our gift to you. We also have other free resources online to help you make progress in pursuing everything God has for you.

Congratulations on your fresh start in your life in Christ! We hope to hear from you soon.

SOURCE NOTES

ABOUT THE AUTHOR

Joyce Meyer is one of the world's leading practical Bible teachers and a *New York Times*–bestselling author. Joyce's books have helped millions of people find hope and restoration through Jesus Christ. Joyce's program, *Enjoying Everyday Life*, is broadcast on television, radio, and online to millions worldwide in over one hundred languages.

Through Joyce Meyer Ministries, Joyce teaches internationally on a number of topics with a particular focus on how the Word of God applies to our everyday lives. Her candid communication style allows her to share openly and practically about her experiences so others can apply what she has learned to their lives.

Joyce has authored more than 140 books, which have been translated into more than 160 languages, and over 39 million of her books have been distributed worldwide. Bestsellers include *Power Thoughts*; *The Confident Woman*; *Look Great, Feel Great*; *Starting Your Day Right*; *Ending Your Day Right*; *Approval*

Addiction; How to Hear from God; Beauty for Ashes; and *Battlefield of the Mind.*

Joyce's passion to help people who are hurting is foundational to the vision of Hand of Hope, the missions arm of Joyce Meyer Ministries. Each year Hand of Hope provides millions of meals for the hungry and malnourished, installs freshwater wells in poor and remote areas, provides critical relief after natural disasters, and offers free medical and dental care to thousands through their hospitals and clinics worldwide. Through Project GRL, women and children are rescued from human trafficking and provided safe places to receive an education, nutritious meals, and the love of God.

JOYCE MEYER MINISTRIES

U.S. & FOREIGN OFFICE ADDRESSES

Joyce Meyer Ministries
P.O. Box 655
Fenton, MO 63026
USA
(636) 349-0303

Joyce Meyer Ministries—Canada
P.O. Box 7700
Vancouver, BC V6B 4E2
Canada
(800) 868-1002

Joyce Meyer Ministries—Australia
Locked Bag 77
Mansfield Delivery Centre
Queensland 4122
Australia
(07) 3349 1200

Joyce Meyer Ministries—England
P.O. Box 1549
Windsor SL4 1GT
United Kingdom
01753 831102

Joyce Meyer Ministries—South Africa
P.O. Box 5
Cape Town 8000
South Africa
(27) 21-701-1056

Joyce Meyer Ministries—Francophonie
29 avenue Maurice Chevalier
77330 Ozoir la Ferriere
France

Joyce Meyer Ministries—Germany
Postfach 761001
22060 Hamburg
Germany
+49 (0)40 / 88 88 4 11 11

Joyce Meyer Ministries—Netherlands
Lorenzlaan 14
7002 HB Doetinchem
+31 657 555 9789

Joyce Meyer Ministries—Russia
P.O. Box 789
Moscow 101000
Russia
+7 (495) 727-14-68

OTHER BOOKS BY JOYCE MEYER

Straight Talk
Strength for Each Day
Teenagers Are People Too!
Trusting God Day by Day
The Word, the Name, the Blood
Woman to Woman
You Can Begin Again
Your Battles Belong to the Lord*

Joyce Meyer Spanish Titles

Auténtica y única (Authentically, Uniquely You)
Belleza en lugar de cenizas (Beauty for Ashes)
Buena salud, buena vida (Good Health, Good Life)
Cambia tus palabras, cambia tu vida
(Change Your Words, Change Your Life)
El campo de batalla de la mente (Battlefield of the Mind)
Cómo envejecer sin avejentarse (How to Age without Getting Old)
Como formar buenos habitos y romper malos habitos
(Making Good Habits, Breaking Bad Habits)
La conexión de la mente (The Mind Connection)
Dios no está enojado contigo (God Is Not Mad at You)
La dosis de aprobación (The Approval Fix)
Efesios: Comentario biblico (Ephesians: Biblical Commentary)
Empezando tu día bien (Starting Your Day Right)
Hágalo con miedo (Do It Afraid)
Hazte un favor a ti mismo…perdona (Do Yourself a Favor…Forgive)
Madre segura de sí misma (The Confident Mom)
Momentos de quietud con Dios (Quiet Times with God Devotional)
Mujer segura de sí misma (The Confident Woman)
No se afane por nada (Be Anxious for Nothing)

Books by Dave Meyer